EXPLORATION AND DISCOVERY

MAIN THEMES IN EUROPEAN HISTORY

Bruce Mazlish, General Editor

Other volumes in preparation

EXPLORATION AND
DISCOVERY

Edited by

ROBERT G. ALBION
Harvard University

THE MACMILLAN COMPANY, NEW YORK
COLLIER-MACMILLAN LIMITED, LONDON

First Printing

Library of Congress catalog card number: 65–15177

The Macmillan Company, New York
Collier-Macmillan Canada, Ltd., Toronto, Ontario

Printed in the United States of America

FOREWORD

History, we are frequently told, is a seamless web. However, by isolating and studying the strands that compose the tapestry of man's past, we are able to discern the pattern, or patterns, of which it is comprised. Such an effort does not preclude a grasp of the warp and woof, and the interplay of the strands; rather, it eventually demands and facilitates such a comprehension. It is with this in mind that the individual volumes of the MAIN THEMES series have been conceived.

The student will discover, for example, that the population changes discussed in one volume relate to the changes in technology traced in another volume; that both changes are affected by, and affect in turn, religious and intellectual developments; and that all of these changes and many more ramify into a complicated historical network through all the volumes. In following through this complex interrelationship of parts, the student recreates for himself the unity of history.

Each volume achieves its purpose, and its appeal to a general audience, by presenting the best articles by experts in the field of history and allied disciplines. In a number of cases, the articles have been translated into English for the first time. The individual volume editor has linked these contributions into an integrated account of his theme, and supplied a selected bibliography by means of footnotes for the student who wishes to pursue the topic further. The introduction is an original treatment of the problems in the particular field. It provides continuity and background for the articles, points out gaps in the existing literature, offers new interpretations, and suggests further research.

The volumes in this series afford the student of history an unusual opportunity to explore subjects either not treated or touched upon lightly in a survey text. Some examples are population—the dramatis personae of history; war—the way of waging peace by other means; the rise of technology and science in relation to society; the role of religious and cultural ideas and institutions; the continuous ebb and flow of exploration and colonialism; and the political and economic works contrived by modern man. Holding fast to these Ariadne threads, the student penetrates the fascinating labyrinth of history.

BRUCE MAZLISH
General Editor

CONTENTS

CONTENTS

INTRODUCTION

The men of the High Renaissance, already exuberant over new achievements in arts and letters, experienced a succession of further thrills around 1500, when news kept arriving of great voyages of discovery. To a Europe that had previously known little beyond its own borders, the world map was suddenly unrolled. In the 30 years between 1492 and 1522, while Leonardo da Vinci, Michelangelo, and Raphael were producing their masterpices and Machiavelli was writing *The Prince,* Christopher Columbus discovered America, Vasco da Gama sailed around the tip of Africa to India, and one of Ferdinand Magellan's ships completed the first circumnavigation of the world by way of South America, the broad Pacific, and the Cape of Good Hope. In those same years, moreover, John Cabot crossed the North Atlantic, Amerigo Vespucci visited South America (and had America named for him), and Vasco Nuñez de Balboa was the first to discover the Pacific, or South Sea as he called it.

That bold voyaging not only gave Europe a strong emotional and intellectual stimulus, but even more important, it paved the way for the remarkable expansion that would spread European influence, through settlement or conquest, over the whole world. As soon as Columbus returned from America, the Pope, a Spanish Borgia, recognized this exploring initiative by granting to Portugal all newly discovered lands to the east of a specific line, and to Spain to the west. Colonies grew up almost immediately in both areas. Then after the defeat of the Spanish Armada in 1588, Holland, England, and France quickly established colonial holdings beyond the seas and engaged in further exploring.

Those famous discoveries were the culmination of a movement launched back around 1415 by a Portuguese prince who became known as Henry the Navigator. Earlier there had been occasional scattered exploration, but most of it was not followed up. The systematic progress of European expansion dates from Henry's determination to penetrate the unknown seas to the southward. He himself did little, if any, navigating, but more than anyone else he promoted exploration. As a matter of semantics, of course, *exploration* means "seeking," and *discovery* means "finding." For every successful discoverer, many explorers, often forgotten, have helped to pave the way. By the time Henry died in 1460, his hardy mariners had rounded the superstition-guarded Cape Bojador, settled the Madeiras, and penetrated part way down the pestilential Guinea Coast. The Portuguese crown continued Henry's questing; by 1488 Bartholomeu Dias had rounded the tip of Africa, which he called the Stormy Cape but which the King changed to Cape of Good Hope. Ten years after that Vasco da Gama completed Henry's dream by continuing on past Good Hope to the Indies, where Portugal would establish its rich eastern empire.

Two prime motives for exploration, frequently present together, have been the hope for national or individual profit, and the gratification of geographical curiosity. Thus, for example, in those voyages around 1500, as well as in many that followed, the chief aim was to find a direct sea route to the spices and silks of the Indies. But along with the profit motive, in many cases there has been the urge of the sailor to know what lay at the end of an ocean crossing or around the next headland, whereas for those who explored ashore, there was similar curiosity about what lay beyond the next mountain range or up the next river.

Exploration, always an expensive activity, has usually been, of course, beyond the resources of the individual; the deep pockets of nations or geographical societies have usually been necessary. It became a standing rule that the country that paid the bills, rather than the nationality of the explorer himself, determined who reaped the major benefits of the voyage. The Italians, the most experienced seamen of that age, operated under various flags—Columbus and Vespucci for Spain, Cadamosto for Portugal, Verrazano for France, and Sebastian Cabot for England, Spain, and then England again. Henry Hudson, an Englishman, was sailing for the Dutch when he discovered the Hudson River and for England when he found Hudson's Bay.

The principal instrument of exploration, developed under Henry the Navigator and continuing for four centuries, was the seagoing sailing vessel, be it caravel, galleon, or any of the other various types. Not until the "marriage" of the sturdy types of Northern Europe with the faster but less seaworthy craft of the Mediterranean did the explorers have a ship that would enable them to make fair progress and keep at sea for months on end. It was that self-contained quality, independent of needs ashore, that made the sailing vessel so indispensable. Even when steam came in during the 1800s, the fact that it could push a little better through polar ice was offset by the fact that out at the ends of the earth there was seldom a chance to replenish a coal supply. It was only with the twentieth century that the airplane would become the exploring instrument par excellence. In the meantime, for several centuries the sailing vessels participated in the major exploration and discovery. For one thing, it was far easier to be carried by sea than to struggle through jungle, wilderness, or desert ashore.

In the selections that follow, we shall find accounts of Prince Henry and the "big three"—Columbus, da Gama, and Magellan. Although their early achievements revealed the major outlines of world geography, much else remained to be done, both by land and by sea. But there is no room here to follow this last in detail, even though some of the later findings did pave the way for important historical results.

Although the Portuguese and Spaniards continued to carry on some further exploring, the principal additional findings in the decades just before and after 1600 came from the English and the Dutch. Many of these mariners were not explorers pure and simple; fighting, trading, and colonizing were all mixed in with their search for new places. For a brief while, they pushed Arctic exploration vigorously in the hope of discovering a Northeast or Northwest passage to the Spice Islands that would be beyond the reach of the Portuguese and the Spaniards, who controlled the routes by Good Hope and by the Straits of Magellan, respectively. Ice, however, blocked the top of Asia and America; and once the Spanish Armada had been smashed, it was possible to go to the East by Good Hope. Yet the quest for the Northwest Passage did much to stimulate the exploration of North America—the voyagers went up river after river hoping that China was just around the bend. The Dutch, in their great half-century between 1600 and 1650, prowled all the seas in their quest for profits. In the course of that prowl, Abel Tasman discovered Australia and New Zealand, but the Dutch did not follow it up, because it promised scant profit.

The impact of that early exploration upon the minds and imaginations of Europe was reflected in the literature of the day. One outstanding single work was *The Lusiads,* a stirring epic of Portugal's maritime activity in the East, written in the mid-1500s by Luis Vaz de Camoëns during his adventurous decades out there. So, too, the exploits of the Elizabethan "sea dogs" aroused a wide interest and broadening of horizons that found their way into the literature of the day. Shakespeare and Marlowe each devoted a whole play to the

subject as well as numerous scattered allusions. The name most
closely associated with early exploration, however, is that of Richard
Hakluyt, a Cambridge-trained, clergyman-geographer who collected
all the explorers' tales he could, feeling that they should be preserved
to gratify the widespread national enthusiasm for such achievements.
Just before 1600 he produced his multivolume *Principal Navigations,
Voyages and Discoveries of the English Nation;* before this he had
already written effective propaganda for the settlement of America.
(In his honor and to carry on his work, the Hakluyt Society was formed
in 1846 to edit, translate if necessary, and print "the most rare and
valuable voyages, travels, and geographical records"; it has published
more than 200 volumes.)

By the eighteenth century, scientific inquiry was becoming linked
with exploration and was to stimulate many voyages, especially in the
little known Pacific. Foremost among these were those of a gifted
scientist, the French explorer, Louis de Bougainville, 1766–69, and the
more celebrated Captain James Cook of the British Navy. The latter's
three famous voyages between 1768 and 1779 really made the world
"Pacific-conscious". They are the only post-Magellan cases of maritime
exploration included here. It was significant that Sir Joseph Banks, an
amateur scientist and later head of the Royal Society, helped promote
Cook's project and went along on the first voyage. The interest continued, not fully concerned with finding new places, but also with
their flora, fauna, and other aspects. Thus, Charles Darwin, the British
scientist, began to work up his evolution theory, while on a far-ranging
cruise in H.M.S. *Beagle,* 1831–36. Then, the United States Navy sent
an exploring expedition, 1839–42, under Lieutenant Charles Wilkes; it
gathered quantities of scientific data in the Pacific and at the edge of
Antarctica, along with preparing charts of Pacific islands and atolls that
the United States Navy would use with relatively little change a century
later in World War II. One of the most important scientific-maritime
expeditions was that of H.M.S. *Challenger,* sent out jointly by the
Admiralty and the Royal Society, with an unusually capable group
of scientists aboard, who turned in a 50-volume report. A steam cruiser,
but under sail most of the time, she was at sea from December 1872 to
May 1876. Visiting many parts of the oceans, she built up a volume
of data on temperatures, currents, depths, contours, and marine biology
that laid the fountain of the science of oceanography.

While all this was going on at sea, explorers were also penetrating
the mysteries of the interiors of the new found continents. In North
America the Spaniards ventured through much of the south and the

southwest; Coronado and others were hunting rumors of gold; Ponce de Leon was seeking the fountain of youth; and DeSoto reached the lower Mississippi. In the seventeenth century the French did much to reveal the mysteries of the great rivers and lakes of the interior, particularly La Salle, who explored the Mississippi and its tributaries; that is the one portion of the American exploration that we have included here. Later the Scot Alexander Mackenzie and the United States army officers Lewis and Clark crossed the whole continent to the Pacific.

Probably the most important interior exploration, from the standpoint of historical development, was the sudden unveiling of the mysteries of the interior of Africa, the Dark Continent. Its coastline had been known to the Europeans, of course, since the days of the Portuguese explorers, but there had been scant interest in penetrating the generally pestilential interior. The great work in this field was accomplished by a group of Britons in the mid-nineteenth century. Baker, Speke, and Burton explored the upper Nile, and even more important, a Scottish missionary, David Livingstone, investigated the Zambesi and parts of East Africa. An Anglo-American journalist, Henry M. Stanley, not only traced the route of the Congo but also wrote of it in a fashion that made the world "Africa-conscious" and helped precipitate the scramble that quickly divided the continent among the European imperialistic powers.

In the meantime several national geographical societies were being organized to promote and publicize exploration and discovery. In Britain the Royal Geographical Society had been first formed in 1830 and incorporated in 1859. Its "fellows," who had geographical achievements to their credit, were proud to add the initials "F.R.G.S." after their names. Similar societies developed in other countries, for example, in the United States, the American and National Geographical Societies issued journals that made the public aware of new developments in the field.

After the early Arctic quests for the Northeast and Northwest passages around 1600, interest in the polar regions had pretty much quieted down until the early nineteenth century, when it suddenly revived in 1818. The next 40 years saw more than 60 expeditions, with few tangible accomplishments. In 1878 a Swedish baron, Nils Nordenskjöld, first traversed the Northeast Passage from Europe to the Pacific in his ship *Vega*. The Northwest Passage was first negotiated by Roald Amundsen, a Norwegian, in his *Gjoa* in 1903–1906. Close upon the latter came the discovery of the North Pole by an American naval officer, Robert E. Peary, in 1909. Two years later the versatile Amundsen discovered the South Pole, just a month ahead of a British naval officer, Robert Scott, who perished in returning.

A new instrument that tremendously accelerated exploring efforts was the airplane. When, in 1928, the Australian Hubert Wilkins, later Sir Hubert, flew over considerable parts of the Arctic and Antarctic, it was said that he "recorded more in hours than his predecessors were able to do in years." Shortly after that an American naval officer, Richard E. Byrd, flew over both the North and South Poles. From that time on, airplane polar exploration became quite frequent.

As early as 1882–1883 ten nations had participated in an International Polar Year. Far more important and comprehensive was the practically world-wide organization of an International Geophysical Year in 1957–1958. This led to particularly valuable cooperative results in the Antarctic, where the United States Navy has conducted expeditions year after year. Part of the twentieth-century polar story is covered here in the popular article by Lowell Thomas, who seems to have provided a more convenient treatment of a half century of exploration than anyone else.

In contrast to the quest for new areas that did not "pay," there has been the twentieth-century search for oil in regions already known. With the rapid development of the internal combustion engine, particularly in automobiles, the demand for oil has grown to tremendous proportions. This has been highly profitable for the regions where oil has been found in quantity. The United States, Venezuela, and the Middle East have been the leading producers, and continual exploration keeps revealing new areas. This is a particular instance in which only a small fraction of the explorers achieve success as discoverers. Our article on this subject is written by one of the most successful of the latter.

Back in the Elizabethan days, literature followed after the achievements of the explorers, but in the latest phase of exploration, the reverse has been true, From Jules Verne onward, writers of science fiction have been developing heroes who ventured into what seemed fantastic and utterly unreal experiences in outer space. Since World War II, however, actual exploration has been accomplishing wonders in this field. Rocket-launched satellites and missiles have been propelled into outer space. Human astronauts have been carried several times around the earth beyond its normal atmosphere. Missiles have been sent to the moon, and plans are afoot to have human astronauts land there. Some of the best scientific minds of the United States and Russia have been striving to outmatch each other in this race, and both nations have spent huge sums; the United States' bill has come to some 20 billion already and may rise to 30 or more by the time the astronauts reach the moon. Though some voice skepticism as to the value of such efforts, others hope to go on still further, to Mars, to Venus, and to other planets.

It has been possible in this book to include only a few of the major highlights in the story of exporation. Hundreds of other interesting achievements—all the way from those of Henry the Navigator's captains down to the twentieth-century airplane scouting remote deserts and jungles—have had to be omitted for lack of room. At this point in time, however, the surface of the earth has been pretty thoroughly seen from the air, even if men have not set foot on all the more inaccessible places. That is one reason why the exploring urge has now turned toward the outer universe.

NOTES

John N. L. Baker, *A History of Geographical Discovery and Exploration,* London, 1931.

Gerald R. Crone, *Maps and Their Makers,* London, 1953.

Frank Debenham, *Discovery and Exploration: An Atlas History of Man's Journeys into the Unknown,* New York, 1960.

Richard Hakluyt, *The Principal Navigations, Voyages, Traffiques and Discoveries of the English Nation,* London, 1598–1600.

Edward Heawood, *A History of Geographical Discovery in the Seventeenth and Eighteenth Centuries,* Cambridge, Eng., 1912.

John H. Parry, *The Age of Reconnaissance,* London, 1963.

Boies Penrose, *Travel and Discovery in the Renaissance,* Cambridge, Mass., 1955.

Raleigh A. Skelton, *Explorers' Maps: Chapters in the Cartographic Record of Geographical Discovery,* London, 1958.

Sir Percy Sykes, *A History of Exploration from the Earliest Times to the Present Day,* London, 1934.

WHEREIN LIES THE INTEREST
IN GEOGRAPHICAL EXPLORATION? *

John K. Wright

Every reader, mature or immature, probably relishes records of exploration partly for what they tell of lands and seas and peoples, either as they are today or used to be in the past. Scientists and scholars pore over them to glean factual data for very diverse purposes—as, for example, when historians ransacked the narratives of explorations· in connection with the inflammatory boundary dispute of 1897 between Venezuela and Great Britain, or when the late Professor Lowes dug deep into the literature of maritime voyages in search of the origins of the imagery in *Kubla Khan* and *The Ancient Mariner*. In order to plan their journeys, explorers examine the records to ascertain what may already by known about the approaches to unknown areas and what can be surmised about their interiors. Here, exploration will be considered as a major form of human activity, of which the development is of interest from the historical, the geographical, and the psychological points of view.

The reader with historical tastes views exploration as motivated by and as affecting larger movements and events. "From the earliest times to the present day" exploration has been impelled by one or the other or both of two purposes: to discover and to bridge gaps. The discovery motive is the urge to open up the unknown for exploitation or trade, conquest or settlement, or for the satisfaction of curiosity, idle or scientific; the gap-bridging motive is the urge to establish contacts *across* the unknown, friendly or hostile, with other centers of civilization or wealth or power that lie beyond. . . . Scientific exploration, which had its inception on a large scale during the last half of the seventeenth century, no less than exploration for more mundane purposes is impelled by these same two motives.

The impact of exploration upon the larger course of history is so vast a subject that only a hint can be given of its scope and shape. Whether recorded or forgotten in the mists of time, exploration has

* Introduction by John K. Wright in Torchbook edition of Sir Percy Sykes, *A History of Exploration from the Earliest Times to the Present Day* (New York: Harper & Row, 1961), pp. xiv–xxii. Copyright © 1961 by John K. Wright.

nearly everywhere prepared the way for conquest, settlement, and the setting up of economic and political enterprises and institutions—it has been the prelude to the birth of cultures and of nations. Also, long after a nation's own home land has been explored, exploration beyond its borders may vitally affect the lives and fortunes of its people and institutions—witness what the explorations and discoveries of the sixteenth century did for Spain and Portugal and Britain. Whole edifices of science and literature and art have been erected out of building materials in the form of facts and ideas gathered by exploring expeditions. A fascinating and enduring, if minor, effect of exploration is the legacy of place names bestowed by explorers. Among the oldest of these, no doubt, is "Kandahar," a corruption of "Alexandria," the name bestowed during Alexander the Great's expedition upon no fewer than ten towns; among the most recent are "Executive Committee Range" and "International Geophysical Year Valley" in Antarctica. In the Polar Regions the clusterings of names of different types proclaim the nationalities of the first explorers, and the commemorative names of emperors and empresses, kings and queens, princes and princesses, explorers' wives and millionaires proclaim loyalties at the time of exploration. The diversity of the polar "place-name cover" is almost as revealing of the history of exploration as the vegetation cover, photographed from the air, is of the history of land use.

The geographically-minded reader looks to the records of exploration for the light that they can shed upon relationships between the process of exploration, on the one hand, and the geographic environment or the historical study of geography, on the other. How specific elements of the geographic environment—winds, deserts, mountains, people, fanaticism—may help or hinder, attract or repel, exploration will be illustrated a little later. Here it should be noted that, while in general the environmental conditions that attract exploration also favor it, the reverse is sometimes the case: many a venturesome and ascetic explorer disdains the easy, pleasant route, preferring the hard way through the steaming tangles of an equatorial rain forest, or across burning sands, or by stony trails on windswept heights. . . .

The historical study of geography is the study of either actual geographic circumstances or of geographical ideas, as they both were in the past. The former study, usually called "historical geography," aims to reconstruct and interpret such things as the distribution of forests and crop land in Roman Britain, or medieval trade routes, or changing patterns of political jurisdiction as shown on maps. The latter, known as the "history of geography," aims to trace the development of geographical knowledge in all its ramifications. For both types of study, the records of exploration are invaluable as sources of information. The history of exploration is part and parcel of the history of geography. . . . The explorer is always impelled to seek or avoid the unknown by preconceived notions regarding its nature, and these notions are derived in part from borrowed or inherited geographical knowledge or lore, true or false. The study of how such knowledge has affected and in turn has been affected by the actual course of exploration leads into enthralling and little-explored regions in the history of ideas.

Explorations in various types of country and for different purposes are endowed in varying degress with physical, vegetal, animal, and human interest, depending on what the explorers observe and on what they do. Antarctic exploration, for example, is totally devoid of human interest in the matter of what the explorers observe (except concerning one another); it is almost without vegetal or animal interest (other than that concerning a few lichens, penguins, and dogs), but it is replete with physical interest. The last, moreover, is true of all polar, high-mountain, and oceanic exploration, the locales of which, by and large, though they attract the physical and biological scientists, have little or nothing to offer their colleagues in the social sciences and humanities. Hence the geographic environment tends to exert a selective influence upon explorers, and this, in turn, is reflected in the general tone—the prevailing philosophical and literary quality—of the "literature" of the exploration of different regions. It is no accident that in most books on polar exploration and mountaineering the emphasis is predominantly upon physical facts or inferences and upon physical adventure, nor that a disproportionately large fraction of the works on exploration that seem to endure as literary classics have had to do with journeys in the ancient lands of the Middle East.

With regard to exploration as an activity, the vegetal, animal, and physical interests relate, of course, to problems of logistics—to food supply, beasts of burden or of traction, vehicles, and so forth. Whereas the old-style explorer's narrative had much to say of dogs or horses, camels or yaks, today we are likely to read of machines and how they function and in particular of the endless tinkering they require. Old-style exploration placed a premium on veterinarian, new-style on mechanical skill. The human interest in exploration as an activity is primarily psychological.

Down the ages the most powerful personal impulses that have led men into exploration have probably been such motives as patriotism, loyalty to king or country, ambition to achieve glory or fame or wealth, and, latterly, interest in a particular branch of science. It has also often been said that explorers are attracted by an irresistible urge to penetrate the unknown, and that the more unknown, difficult, and hostile it may seem, the more powerful its lure. But, while undoubtedly many explorers have been attracted in this way and have so testified in their own writings in words that have the ring of sincere conviction, it should also be noted that it is "the thing" on the part of explorers, these days, to experience such an emotion and that some of the glamor that explora-tion has acquired during the past 150 years or so may have sprung from literary romanticism and journalism.

On the behavior of explorers under the stress and strain of explora-tion, the narratives of expeditions shed a little light, and, with the development of modern psychology and psychiatry it has even been made the subject of experimental research. Broadly, there are two interesting sides of the subject: that of the behavior of the individual explorer when in isolation from his kind and that of the group cooped up for a long time in a ship or isolated encampment. Paul Siple in his account of the first winter spent by men at the South Pole tells amus-ingly of how the young scientists, though in deadly earnest about the conduct of their own scientific programs, responded to efforts to use them as psychological guinea-pigs by giving fantastic answers to ques-tionaires sent out by psychologists in the United States.

Exploration lies midway between war and "show business" and partakes of some of the characteristics of each. Like war, its ultimate purpose is achievement rather than entertainment and, as in war, endurance, suffering, and genuine tragedy are inherent in it. Unlike modern war, however, exploration resembles show business in that participation in it is voluntary and therefore selective of individuals who enjoy adventure and the heroic. Furthermore, in their wide range of size and variety, exploring expeditions are comparable to shows. The lone explorer has his counterpart in the monologist or concert pianist; the college and university-sponsored expeditions are analogous to ama-teur college dramatics; the small, highly specialized and professionally competent scientific expedition corresponds to a sucessful play on Broadway; a "Highjump" or a "Deepfreeze" to a colossal spectacle of Cecil B. De Mille; [1] and there have even been exploratory circuses, melodramas, and soap operas. The behavior of an occasional explorer after returning home has sometimes been not unlike that of a screen star or prima donna, not only in that the explorer performs before large audiences but in other ways. In one respect, however, exploration is totally different from the performing arts and in the same class as the regal, legal, military, and ministerial professions: traditionally, it

---

[1] "Highjump" and "Deepfreeze" were elaborate United States operations in the Antarctic.

has been almost exclusively a masculine affair, although as in these other professions, a few rare women have greatly distinguished themselves in it—notably, Mary Kingsley in Africa, Gertrude Bell, Rosita Forbes, and Freya Stark in Asia, and Louise A. Boyd in the Arctic. Miss Boyd has financed, organized, and led no fewer than eight Arctic expeditions, and in recognition thereof was the first woman to be elected to membership in the Council of the American Geographical Society, some 108 years after the founding of that institution. The paucity of women, however, has almost completely deprived the history of exploration of sexual interest, thus rendering it a more suitable concern for the young and innocent than the history of show business would be.

.   .   .   .

Unexplored and Explored

Since there is little consistency in the use of terms regarding concepts essential to an understanding of the history of exploration, we must venture for a moment upon the quaking quicksands of semantics. For present working purposes, let me suggest that areas be classed as either unexplored, sub-explored, or explored, and that primary exploration be defined as the process whereby the unexplored is converted into the sub-explored, and secondary exploration as that which converts the sub-explored into the explored or the explored into the even more intensively explored. The unexplored might be defined as consisting of unseen, unphotographed, and unmapped areas on the earth's surface for which no observed facts whatsoever are on record on maps or in scientific publications (as thus defined, the largest unexplored area in 1959 was in East Antarctica; it was somewhat more than twice the size of Texas). Sub-explored areas might be regarded as consisting either of a patchwork of small explored and unexplored tracts, or of areas of which the exploration, though comprehensive, has been inadequate in that it has yielded relatively little new geographical knowledge. In this latter category would fall areas that have been merely "eye-explored" (seen from afar), or "photo-explored" without sufficient ground control, or else "ground-explored," but inadequately because the explorer was untrained or unable to make reasonably complete and accurate observations or failed to do so because he was more intent upon adventure or other business. Where to draw the line between the sub-explored and the explored is a delicate question, which need not be answered here. The point of this discussion is to illustrate rather than to apply general principles.

It should be noted that "unexplored" is not synonymous with "unknown," nor "explored" with "known." In general, today we know a good deal about unexplored areas from inference, and the smaller they are the more we know. Thus we know as indisputably as anything can be known, that the climate is cold and windy in the unexplored parts of southern Patagonia and that there are no alligators or hippopotami in the rivers there. Indeed, exploredness and unexploredness, knownness and unknownness, like cold and heat are better regarded as relatives and not as absolutes, and their different degrees as depending upon our standards of judgment and scales of reference. If there is, perhaps, an absolute zero of unknownness, there seems practically no limit beyond which the mind cannot produce knownness, and a geographer in 2960 A.D. may well look back upon our vaunted geographical knowledge of, say, the Middle West, as "medieval" and not far removed from total ignorance. Also, naturally, the larger the scale upon which an area is mapped or described, the more in evidence become the gaps in the information so set forth: on a small-scale atlas map Borneo or Patagonia look as well known as does California, but compare them on large-scale maps and you will see a great difference.

The progressive shrinkage of the unexplored areas has had a twofold effect upon the nature of exploration. In the first place, by rendering them better known from inference, it has reduced the possibility of discoveries of any consequence within them except on the part of scientifically-trained explorers. In the old days almost any bold adventurer, however ill-equipped with instruments and skills, could bring back valuable, albeit inexact, information about unknown mountain ranges, plains, lakes, rivers, cities, and other major features of the landscape. Today this is next to impossible, and the untrained explorer is of little use to anybody—unless, of course, he has a facile pen or eloquent tongue.

In the second place, the diminution in size of the unexplored areas combined with greatly increased speed of travel has largely done away with the long and lonely journeys that furnished much of the adventure of earlier exploration and called upon the endurance, fortitude, and heroism of the old-time explorers. "Expeditions with specialists intensively studying a limited area" have become "the order of the day." The typical expedition of the 1950's sojourns for one or more seasons at a base camp, from which its members make excursions of greater or lesser distances (but increasingly "lesser") for geographical surveying and the making of other scientific observations. Sir Vivian Fuchs' trans-Antarctic journey of 1957–1958 was, indeed, carried out in the grand manner of the greatest polar journeys, but even so it took only a little more than three months, as compared with the thirty-five months of the *Fram* drift (1893–1896) [2] and the fourteen during which Nansen and Johansen were alone after leaving their little vessel.

BACKGROUND, CLASSICAL AND MEDIEVAL *

Boies Penrose

It is probable that until the middle of the thirteentth century no European had traveled east of Baghdad. Undoubtedly the Crusades had given many men some knowledge of Syria, Palestine, and even Asia Minor, while there had always been a certain amount of pilgrimage travel to Jerusalem. But the farther Orient had remained cut off, until an event, or rather a series of events, opened up literally a limitless vista to the East. Early in the thirteenth century Genghis Khan established his authority over the Mongols in Central Asia and after subduing China, embarked on a campaign of wider conquests to the West, which actually carried him across South Russia into Poland. After the first fury of the Tatar conquest had spent itself, Genghis and his successors settled down to the consolidation of their vast domains, which stretched from the Dneister to the Pacific, and showed themselves as sage in peace as they had been terrible in war. They tolerated Christians in their dominions and even welcomed European traders; while the administration of their empire was so efficient that travelers could cross the vast expanses of Central Asia with ease and safety. A phenomenon had thus come about such as the world had not seen since the heyday of the Roman Empire: that of a vast realm, tolerant and well policed, where men of all nations could come and go as they liked. Both missionaries and merchants took advantage of this situation, and for upwards of a century there followed a surprising volume of travel between Western Europe and the further Orient. In 1245 Giovanni

---

* Reprinted by permission of the publishers from Boies Penrose, *Travel and Discovery in the Renaissance 1420–1620*, Cambridge, Mass.: Harvard University Press, Copyright, 1952, 1955, by the President and Fellows of Harvard College. Chap. 1, pp. 14–20.

[2] Fridtjof Nansen, the Norwegian scientist-explorer, in his toughly built *Fram*, drifted westward through the Northeast Passage, firmly held in the ice. He and a Norwegian lieutenant left the drifting ship and started over the ice for the North Pole, reaching 86 degrees, farther north than anyone else had reached.

de Plano Carpini, a Franciscan monk, was sent by the pope on a mission to the Mongol ruler at Karakorum, in a remote district of Asia between the Gobi Desert and Lake Baikal. He was thus the first noteworthy European to explore the Mongol Empire. A similar mission was undertaken, also to Karakorum, by William de Rubruquis in 1253. Some years after these ventures the Mongol rulers removed their capital to Cambaluc (Peking), which remained their principal residence during the period of the other European visits. Kublai Khan, the celebrated Oriental potentate of song and story, was ruling there when the first commercial travelers from the West reached Cathay. These courageous businessmen were the two brothers Polo, merchants of Venice, who traveled overland to China about 1256 and remained in Kublai's new capital nearly fourteen years. After an absence in Europe they were back again with young Marco—destined to become one of the greatest travelers of all time. They had spent four years on the return trip to China, journeying through Persia and the Pamirs and across northern Tibet, and they were fated to remain in China seventeen more years before returning to their native Venice. During these years Marco was admitted to the diplomatic service of the khan, and in consequence was able to travel widely through Kublai's dominions. In 1292 the Polos started homeward, proceeding by sea along the coasts of the Malay Peninsula, Sumatra, and India; they reached Venice three years later. Marco Polo was succeeded by a number of travelers, of whom ecclesiastics were the most prominent. To name but a few who made their way to China early in the fourteenth century, there were Giovanni de Monte Corvino, Odoric of Pordenone, Andrew of Perugia, Jordan of Severac, and Giovanni de Marignolli. Most of these men made protracted stays on the Indian coast on the way. Compared with them the itinerant merchants are garbed in anonymity, except for the Polos, but that there were a fair number is evidenced by the survival of a highly interesting manuscript (in the Riccardian Library, Florence) by one Francesco Pegolotti, an agent of the great Florentine house of Bardi. This is nothing less than a handbook of the route to be followed in traveling form the Levant to Peking; it includes the stages of the journey and means of transport, the most suitable articles of commerce for the Chinese trade, and the profits most likely to accrue. It further contains the comforting assurance that the road is perfectly safe, whether by day or by night.

This happy state lasted until the middle of the fourteenth century, when several events effectively disrupted it, at least as far as Cathay and Central Asia were concerned. First, the terrible plague known as the Black Death swept Europe in 1348–1349 and shook the medieval world to its foundations; second, the rise of the Ottoman Turks interposed a barrier between East and West; third, the beneficent Tatar Empire ended its sway in China when the descendants of Kublai Khan were driven from his brilliant capital in 1368. In consequence, intercourse with China ended for almost two hundred years, and when at length the Portuguese reached the Celestial Empire, it was almost as if they had made a discovery similar to that of Cortes in Mexico. Yet, the memory of the medieval journeys lived on, and the number of surviving manuscripts and incunabula editions shows how popular this literature was in pre-Columbian as well as Columbian times. Judged on this basis, the *Travels of Marco Polo* was by all odds the most popular and most influential book of the type, being represented by at least 138 manuscripts still in existence. Of the early printed editions, that by Leeu of Gouda, 1483–1485 (Hain 13244), was owned by Columbus, and is preserved in the Columbina in Seville. It was issued as a companion volume to the same printer's *Mandeville* . . . which in all probability Columbus therefore had also. Second in popularity to Polo's *Travels* was the *Descriptio Orientalium Partium* of Odoric of Pordenone, with at least seventy-three surviving manuscript texts: it forms a valuable supplement to Polo's book, even though the friar could not avoid the legendary atmosphere, which Mandeville found useful in his plagiarizing. Manuscripts remaining from the other missioners are fewer in number; perhaps one or two apiece for each traveler. But the strategic-religious *Crusaders' Manual* of Marino Sanuto, a Venetian statesman and political writer, and the *Itinerario* of Ricold of Monte Croce, a hot-Gospeller who traveled in Persia and Iraq preaching to the Moslems in their own language, survive in considerable quantity. From this it is obvious that the medieval tradition of Asiatic land travel lived on, and even though Pierre d'Ailly never heard of Marco Polo, we know that Polo's geographical information went where it counted most. Abraham Cresques used it in compiling the *Catalan Atlas*, Henry the Navigator had a manuscript of it, and Columbus had a printed edition.

In the Mediterranean the trade with the Orient was mostly in the hands of the Venetians and the Genoese, whose power and prosperity had grown enormously during the Crusades. Venice backed the Latins when they captured Constantinople on the Fourth Crusade in 1204, and profited greatly during the period of the Latin Emperors. Genoa, on the other hand, supported the Byzantines, and rode into power when the Palaeologi were restored in 1261. This had the result of making the Genoese supreme in Constantinople in the later Middle Ages. From there they extended their activities to the Black Sea, the Caspian Sea, and northern Persia. At Kaffa in the Crimea they controlled a flourishing city the size of Seville; at Tana near the mouth of the River Don they had a powerful station for southern Russia and Turkestan; they were strongly entrenched at Trebizond, where a romantic empire of the Byzantine Comneni endured until its capture by the Ottomans in 1461. Farther east, their shipping was seen on the Caspian before the end of the thirteenth century, and they had valuable trading privileges in Tabriz, whither the Englishman Walter Langley went in 1291—the first of his race to reach the Middle East. This Central Asian trade of the Genoese persisted long after the breakup of the Mongol Empire. In Africa, too, the Genoese were active, and there is evidence that they got up the Nile as far as Dongola in the Sudan. From their factory in Tunis they penetrated into the Sahara; Antonio Malfante in 1447 went far into the desert and wrote a description of the Niger basin. The dynamic activity of this Italian city-state even took its sailors into the Atlantic, and in 1291 two Genoese brothers, Guido and Ugolino Vivaldo, sought with magnificent daring to do at one stroke what later took the Portuguese almost a century. With the intention of reaching India by the Cape route, the brothers sailed boldly into the Atlantic— and were never heard of again. It is generally accepted, too, that Genoese-Portuguese expeditions discovered Madeira and the Azores in the mid-fourteenth century. These early Atlantic voyages seem to have been sporadic ventures, however, which were not followed up and were soon forgotten about; what evidence there is for their existence is mostly from portolan charts.

Beside the far-flung commercial activity of Genoa, the trafficking even of Venice seems rather secondary, yet the Venetians can in no way be ignored. They suffered considerably when the Latins fell and the Byzantines were restored in Constantinople, but they continued to maintain a respectable share of the Black Sea trade, with agencies at Kaffa, Tana, and Trebizond. In the western Mediterranean they were less active, sending but one fleet a year to North Africa. In fact, Venice's policy became more and more one of concentration, just as Genoa's had became more and more one of dispersion; and the Venetians established a monopoly amounting to a stranglehold on the Egyptian trade. The Adriatic, the Archipelago, Alexandria—this was Venice's life line, and she tended to pass over the possibility of trade elsewhere in order to keep this immensely valuable monopoly. The Egyptian trade was in a larger sense the trade of Southern Asia and the East Indies: cargoes came from the Spice Islands to Malacca, from Malacca to Calicut, from Calicut to Suez, and from Suez they were laden in Venetian bottoms at Alexandria. This trade supplied more and more of the bulk of Venetian activity and serves to explain why Venetian citizens like

Nicolo Conti and John Cabot penetrated into the Orient in the fifteenth century.

Other Mediterranean peoples were active in those days, especially the seamen of Marseilles and Catalonia. They bore some part of the Black Sea trade and a considerable share of the North African commerce. The Catalans, in particular, made valuable contributions to nautical science, and like the Genoese were tempted by the waters of the Atlantic. An expedition, led by Jaime Ferrer, daringly set forth in 1346 to find the River of Gold. Like the venture of the Vivaldi it was never heard of again, although the *Catalan Atlas* shows Ferrer's craft heading into the unknown off Cape Bojador. Even the seafaring Normans felt the urge of discovery, and the voyage of Bethencourt and Gadifer to the Canary Islands in 1402 brings the chronicle of medieval voyaging up to the very days of Henry the Navigator.

In the same year that the French were accomplishing the conquest of the Canaries, another of their race broke fresh ground in West Africa: an adventurous citizen of Toulouse, Anselme d'Isalguier, crossed the Sahara Desert to the semibarbaric metropolis of Gao, situated on the Niger two hundred miles east of Timbuctoo. It must have been a very courageous undertaking to cross hundreds of miles of desert with hostile Moslems in the way. But d'Isalguier succeeded in doing so and remained at Gao for a full decade, finally returning to his native land in 1413 with a half-caste family and a large train of native retainers.

Certain other travelers should not go unnoticed, as knowledge of their journeyings lived after them into the Renaissance. One cannot overlook the Castilian knight Clavijo, who went on a diplomatic mission to the court of Tamerlaine at Samarkand in 1403–1405, or of the German Schiltberger, who was captured at the battle of Nicopolis (1395) and spent years as a prisoner of both Sultan Bayezid and Tamerlaine before regaining his native country.

Discussion of the discoveries of the Norsemen in Greenland, Markland, and Vinland has been omitted here because awareness of them hardly existed outside Scandinavia, while by the fifteenth century even the bare memory of them was so faint that they may be said to have had no influence on Renaissance travel. Greenland alone appears to have been remembered, but was merely regarded as an additional peninsula of Scandinavia, to the north and west of Norway. For purposes of this study, therefore, the Viking voyages may be ignored. Likewise the geographers and explorers of the fifteenth century had no thought of a western continent or New World. Fragmentary remains of the lost Atlantis might persist in the form of mythical islands, but no one expected a land mass of any size between Western Europe and the Far East.

Probably the most complete picture of geographical knowledge as it stood in the later Middle Ages is given in the celebrated *Catalan Atlas,* now preserved in the Bibliotheque Nationale in Paris. . . . This series of maps, made in 1375 by Abraham Cresques, a Jew of Majorca, portrays the world in the light of the travels of Marco Polo and his missionary successors to Cathay, as well as the Venetian and Genoese merchants in the Near and Middle East and North Africa. From the British Isles to the Black Sea, including the Mediterranean, the maps are of the normal portolan type, but of a very high standard. Denmark, the southern parts of Norway and Sweden, and the Baltic Sea are all set out with some accuracy. Northwest Africa is excellent as far as Cape Bojador, but south of that latitude it is conjectural. Thus there is a large lake in the western Sahara, from which one river (the Senegal) flows west into the Atlantic, and another (the Niger) eastward into the Nile. The placing of Tenbuch (Timbuctoo) just north of the lake betrays a knowledge of the Niger basin surprising for the days of Petrarch and Chaucer, but may be the result of information received from Cresques' co-religionists in Morocco. As for Asia, the outline of the Arabian peninsula is roughly correct, although the Persian Gulf is extended too far, making a rather narrow neck of land between Basra and Suez. The Caspian appears in some detail and with considerable knowledge, and the placing of the cities of Central Asia bears witness to a wide familiarity with the writings of Polo and Odoric. India is shown in its true peninsula shape, with the Kingdom of Delhi in the north—and with the mention that Alexander the Great had built many cities thereabout. A large island with a north-south axis named Iana (*sic*) does duty for the Malay Peninsula; it may possibly be meant for Sumatra. Far to the east is the still larger island of Trapobana (*sic,*) which is less easy to classify. China is especially interesting: not only is the semicircular curve of the coastline shown, but the cities immortalized by Polo are all there: Cambaluc (Peking), Zayton (Chang-chow in Amoy harbor), Kinsay (Hank-chow), and other places. Yet even with this remarkable accuracy there is mythical geography as well. Between China and India is the land of pygmies; a blunt and rounded peninsula north of China is the realm of Gog and Magog, with Alexander's wall running from the mountains to the sea (could this be the Great Wall of China?); beyond are the islands of griffons; the sea to the east and south of China is filled with a multitude of small islands, crowded so that they are almost touching. Nevertheless, the

Catalan Atlas is a remarkable production, especially when we consider that it dates more than a century before Columbus and da Gama; there was not another portrayal of the Eastern Hemisphere as well done until the Cantino Map of 1502. It is almost certain, too, that Henry the Navigator saw this atlas or a similar one; for the son of Abraham Cresques was Jahuda Cresques, who, under the name of Master Jacome, was the prince's leading cartographer and navigational expert.

Of equal importance with a knowledge of the globe was a knowledge of navigation. There are three essentials to satisfactory navigation in the open sea: a map to determine the course, a compass to determine the position of North, and an instrument to determine the latitude by fixing the position of the sun or moon. By the year 1400 Western man had reasonably efficient equipment on these scores. In the portolan charts, examples of which date back to about 1300, he had maps of uncanny accuracy. In fact, as far as the Mediterranean coastline goes, they are hardly bettered by the most up-to-date cartography of today. As for the compass, its principle had already been known for perhaps two centuries. In its primitive form it was simply a magnetized needle thrust crosswise through a straw and floated upon a bowl of water, but by 1380 it appeared virtually in its present form, having a revolving card with a north-pointing needle attached to its underside. For position-finding, the astrolabe had been known to the Greeks, and had come down by way of the Arabs to the seafaring population of the Mediterranean. Described simply, the astrolabe consisted of a circular disc, with angles graduated on the rim, and a movable bar, pinioned at the center of the disc, along which the elevation of the sun could be sighted. The angle of the sun with respect to the horizon could then be read off and the latitude computed. A variant of this, especially popular in England, was the cross-staff, which in essence was a primitive quadrant. Tables, computed on the different declinations of the sun for each day of the year, were composed as early as the close of the thirteenth century; they were greatly improved upon by Abraham Zacuto about 1478. As for the actual knowledge of how to sail a boat, the Massiliots, Catalans, and Portuguese had all learned in the tradition passed from the Arabs to the Sicilians in the days of Edrisi, and passed on by the the Sicilians to the Genoese. Thus is was that on the eve of the Renaissance, the maritime people of the Mediterranean and of southwestern Europe had more than a little knowledge of the world and a reasonably fair smattering of navigational skill.

NOTES

R. Beazley, *The Dawn of Modern Geography: A History of Exploration and Geographical Science* (A.D. 300–1420), 3 vols., London, 1896–1906.

Henry H. Hart, *Venetian Adventurer: Being an Account of the Life and Times and of the Book of Messer Marco Polo,* Stanford Univ., 1942.

Gwyn Jones, *The Norse Atlantic Saga: Being the Norse Voyages of Discovery and Settlement to Iceland, Greenland and America,* Oxford, 1964.

THE TOOLS OF THE EXPLORERS *

J. H. Parry

(i) *Charts.* If it was the crusading spirit, in the person of Prince Henry, which set the Portuguese upon a career of overseas expansion, crusading zeal was not, of course, the whole story. Courage, discipline and organizing ability played their part; and besides these moral considerations must be set another group of factors, commercial and above all technical, which contributed to the astonishing achievements of the Portuguese in two continents in the course of a single century. As an introduction to the narrative of Portuguese exploits, some account must be made of these factors; of the tools available in the fifteenth century for making Prince Henry's dreams a reality.

One of the most obvious characteristics of European civilization is its preoccupation with technical problems and its mastery of a wide range of mechanical devices. Technical skill and the ability to turn theoretical knowledge to practical material ends have been major factors in the extension of European influence round the world, and have forcibly, though not always favourably, impressed all the peoples with whom Europeans have come into contact. This characteristic has been most marked in the last century or century-and-a-half; but it has been an important element in the whole history of European expansion. The scientific knowledge of the time, whether the result of genuine discovery or of the revival of classical knowledge, was turned very quickly to practical account.

* J. H. Parry, *The Establishment of the European Hegemony: 1415-1715* (*Europe and the Wider World* in the British edition) (London: Hutchinson & Co., Ltd., 1961), Chap. 1, pp. 13–28. By permission of The Hutchinson Publishing Group.

In the story of exploration and overseas expansion, three branches of technical development proved to be of the first importance. One was the study of geography and astronomy and its application to the problems of practical navigation. The second was ship-building and the development of skill in handling ships. The third was the development of fire-arms and in particular of naval gunnery. In the first two, at least, of these branches of skill the people of Western Europe drew upon the knowledge either of their classical predecessors or of their Eastern neighbours, but applied that knowledge in ways undreamed of by its original discoverers.

It was common knowledge among educated people in the fifteenth century that the earth was round. This, like so much of the academic knowledge of the Middle Ages, was derived at many removes and by devious ways from the Ancients. The Hellenistic world had produced a whole school of systematic mathematicians and cosmographers: Hipparchus, Eratosthenes, Marinus of Tyre, and the geographer Strabo, to mention only the better-known names. Eratosthenes had actually calculated the circumference of the earth and arrived at a surprisingly accurate answer. Both Eratosthenes and Strabo left recognizable descriptions of the continents which they knew. Beyond the limits of the knowledge or report of their own day they were content to leave a blank and to assume a vast encircling ocean. The culmination of ancient geography, however, was in the compilations of the Hellenized Egyptian, Ptolemy, who wrote about A.D. 130, at the time of the greatest extent of the Roman Empire. Ptolemy left two principal works, an Astronomy, more commonly known by its Arabic title, the *Almagest,* and a descriptive *Geography* provided with elaborate maps.

The heirs of the Greeks in geography, as in many other sciences, were the Arabs. Most Arab cosmographers preferred Ptolemy's description of the world to those of his predecessors because it was more complete and more symmetrical. Preoccupied as they were, also, with astronomy and astrology, the Arabs made great use of the *Almagest,* but neglected the *Geography,* which remained a forgotten work throughout most of the Middle Ages. The Arabs added little to geographical knowledge by actual exploration, because their great journeys both by land and by sea were in regions already roughly known to the Ancients—the Mediterranean and the countries bordering the northern Indian Ocean. They believed the Atlantic to be unnavigable, and had a deep superstitious dread of the 'green sea of darkness', which they communicated to Western Europe. On the other hand, Arab geographers contributed a mass of ingenious theory about the hypothetical centre of the habitable world and the symmetrical arrangements of the continents round it. A complex mixture of the *Almagest* and Arab theory, passed on in Latin translation, supplied the basis of academic geography in late mediæval Europe.

Upon this basis European scholastic writers, from Roger Bacon to Pierre d'Ailly, constructed systematic treatises embodying a mass of scriptural references, legends and travelers' tales. Of these works the most influential, and one of the last, was the *Imago Mundi* of Cardinal Pierre d'Ailly, a mine of quotations from Greek, Latin and Arab authorities, a work of immense erudition, but completely remote from sea-faring reality. It is one of the very few books which are known to have been studied by Columbus.

The *Imago Mundi* was written in 1410. That year was notable also for the recovery by Western Europe of Ptolemy's *Geography*, which at last emerged from its long obscurity in the form of a Latin translation. This example of the steady revival of classical learning was obviously of immense significance in the development of scientific geography. It was not, however, an unmixed encouragement to explorers; for though Ptolemy's work was a great improvement upon current theory, it contained a number of ancient errors of fact. Ptolemy's map of the world was a reasonably accurate picture of the Roman Empire and adjacent countries; but outside those limits Ptolemy had filled in the blank spaces of earlier maps from his own imagination. He invented a vast southern continent joined at one end to Africa and at the other to China, making the Indian Ocean a land-locked sea; he declared the whole southern hemisphere to be unnavigable because of the heat; and he contradicted Eratosthenes' estimate of the circumference of the globe, substituting his own, which was an under-estimate of about one-sixth. Ptolemy's *Geography* exercised an immense though not undisputed influence for at least two hundred years; and much of the history of the early discoveries was the story of practical men who proved Ptolemy to be wrong.

From all this it is clear that even the best academic geography of the early fifteenth century bore little relation to the experience of practical sailors. In so far as it was known to seamen at all, it was an almost paralysing discouragement from exploration by sea; and the *mappa-mundi*—the theoretical world-maps based upon it—were useless for the purpose of ocean navigation.

Fifteenth-century sailors, however, did not go to sea without charts. From the thirteenth century at least, there had existed in the Italian and Catalan ports a school of professional hydrographers who drew *portolani*—charts intended for use at sea, based on sailing experience and owing little to academic science. The original designers of these beautiful late mediæval charts are unknown; but the designs were good, and like many devices used by practical men they were repeated, with additions but without fundamental changes, from one generation to another. They consisted of free-hand but clear and accurate outline drawings of coastline with headlands, rivers and harbours marked. The later ones were supplied with compass roses and were criss-crossed with a network of rhumb-lines or loxodromes serving to show the courses from place to place.[1] Most of them covered the Mediterranean and the Black Sea; some extended to northern Europe and included a truncated Africa. They were drawn on a consistent distance scale but not on a consistent projection; it was not until the sixteenth century that Mercator devised his famous projection with its technique of showing both latitude and longitude as straight lines. The working accuracy of the portolans, therefore, was good only for comparatively short passages. They could be used, within limits, for dead-reckoning at sea, but not for fixing the position of a ship out of sight of land.

When the Portuguese embarked on their voyages to the South, charts of the portolan type began to be drawn of the African coast, and it became necessary to have a reference scale against which to mark the features of the coast as they were discovered. In the later fifteenth century, Portuguese cartographers began to add to the network of loxodromes on their charts a single meridian, usually that of Cape St. Vincent, extending across the chart from North to South and marked in degrees of latitude. Latitude could be measured only by celestial observation; and in the early fifteenth century the rudimentary astronomical knowledge of Europe was the preserve of the learned. To the practical sailor it was still a closed book in an unknown language.

The learned world of western Europe derived its knowledge of astronomy from the Arabs, chiefly through Portuguese and Italian Jews, who were the natural intermediaries between Christendom and Islam at that time. The Arabs' purpose in studying the heavens was not primarily navigation, but cosmography and astrology, and for these purposes they relied somewhat uncritically upon Ptolemy's *Almagest* and upon the works of early Indian astronomers. They supplemented Ptolemy, however, by a great deal of painstaking observation spread over many centuries. They identified and named

---

[1] The compass rose or wind rose was a star-shaped device, often very decorative, showing 32 directions from which the winds might blow. "North" came to be marked with a fleur de lis. From various points, rhumb-lines or loxodromes were drawn for the major sea-routes.

many stars and studied their tracks relative to the earth. Some of this astronomical knowledge affected the practice of eastern navigators. Arab sailors regularly sailed by the stars—that is, they shaped their course by the bearings upon which prominent stars were known to rise and set. Such a system was reliable only in the latitudes where no great variation occurred in the azimuths of the appropriate stars, and where the regularity of the seasonal winds made it possible to sail great distances upon a prearranged course. Some Arab *baghlas* cross the Indian Ocean in the same manner to-day. What was more important, fifteenth-century Arab sailors posseessed rough methods of observing the altitude of heavenly bodies as a help in fixing their position. Portuguese navigators, in solving far more difficult problems than the Arab sailor ever had to face, needed similar help from the men of science. One of the tasks of Prince Henry and his successors was to bring together for this purpose the seafaring and the learned worlds of Europe.

The easiest and most obvious star to use in observing latitude is the Pole Star, because it is always aligned within a few degrees of the earth's axis. The altitude of the Pole Star—the vertical angle between the star and the observer's horizon—gives the observer's latitude. The first recorded observation of latitude from the altitude of the Pole Star in a European ship was in 1462, two years after Prince Henry's death, but there is no doubt that his captains had been experimenting with the method for some years before that. As exploration went on, however, the Pole Star sank towards the horizon; and as they approached the equator the explorers lost sight of it altogether. The difficulty of observing latitude in the southern hemisphere was a serious stumbling-block to fifteenth-century navigators; but in 1484 a group of astronomers consulted by King John II produced the suggestion that latitude might be calculated from observation of the height of the sun at midday. For this calculation, the navigator would need tables of the sun's declination—the distance of the sun's zenith north or south of the equator at noon on any given day. Here the Arab study of the heavens was of use, again through the medium of the Jews. An almanac containing declination tables had been compiled in 1478 by a Portuguese Jew named Abraham Zacuto, who was professor of astronomy at Salamanca, and who later, upon the expulsion of the Jews from Spain, came to Lisbon as astronomer-royal. Zacuto's tables were written in Hebrew. John II's committee had them translated into Latin, and shortly afterwards (the date is uncertain) they were published in Portuguese as part of a general treatise on navigation entitled *O Regimento do Astrolabio*. The publication of this, the first practical manual, marked a revolutionary advance in the science of navigation.

It is characteristic of the Portuguese attitude that they did not neglect to send an expedition to Guinea in 1485 to test the new methods of observing latitude.

To sum up: at the beginning of the fifteenth century the navigator had no means of finding his position once he lost sight of land, and consequently he took care as a rule not to lose sight of land. At the end of the century, an intelligent and literate navigator had at his disposal several methods of discovering his latitude; he had an agreed estimate of the geographical length of a degree of latitude—eighteen Portuguese leagues, an error of only four per cent; and he had charts on which his observations could be plotted. He had no meeans of finding his longitude—that was a more difficult problem, not satisfactorily solved until the eighteenth century; but by a combination of observed latitude and dead-reckoning he could keep track of his position tolerably well. Much of the mediæval navigator's horror of the open sea had thus been dissipated. All this achievement was due to an unprecedented combination of sea experience and academic knowledge; and the methods really worked. In Vasco da Gama's great voyage to India, which closed the century, there was no more dramatic feature than the accuracy of his navigation and of his first landfall on the South African coast.

It would be wrong, however, to assume that even at the end of the century the taking of celestial observations was a commonplace among sailors. On the contrary, it was a considerable event, and when successful was recorded with pride in the journals of voyages. Celestial navigation did not yet form part of the professional training of ships' officers, and even practised experts needed favourable conditions in order to achieve reliable results.

A word about instruments: European ships had carried compasses at least since the thirteenth century, and by Prince Henry's day the compass had developed from a magnetized needle floating on a chip of wood in a bowl of water, to a pivoted needle swinging above a compass-card marked with the four cardinal 'winds' and the thirty-two points which we know. Gimbals were introduced about 1500.[2] The existence of variation was known, but the extent of variation in different longitudes was a matter of conjecture. The compass gave the navigator his course to steer, and from a sketchy knowledge of ocean currents he estimated his course made good. Speed made good was largely a matter of guess-work. The earliest form of log was a

[2] Gimbals were rings supporting the compass.

piece of wood, made fast to a long line knotted at regular intervals; when the log was streamed, the speed at which the knots ran out over the stern was timed with a diminutive sand-glass. This 'chip' log, however, was an early sixteenth-century invention; in the fifteenth century, the navigator studied the behaviour of his ship along known stretches of coast, and so learned to guess his speed by watching bits of wood or other flotsam floating by. For dead-reckoning, he used a chart of the kind already described, usually drawn on parchment. He had no pencil, and pricked holes in the chart with his dividers instead—as slovenly navigators still do. Having no parallel ruler, he lined up his straight-edge with the nearest convenient loxodrome on the chart.

For celestial navigation the principal requirement was an instrument for measuring the altitude of heavenly bodies. The cross-staff and its refinement the back-staff were sixteenth-century instruments; the standard fifteenth-century device was the astrolabe. The elaborate brass astrolabes, both oriental and European, which survive in many museums, were designed to work out a variety of academic astronomical and astrological problems, and were probably never used at sea. The astrolabes actually used by the Portuguese navigators were much simpler, the simplest form being a disc marked in degrees with a swivelling pointer mounted at the centre. The pointer was fitted with aperture sights, one at each end. The instrument was suspended vertically from a ring at the top. The observer held the ring in his left hand, and with his right aligned the sights with his chosen star. He then read off the angle shown by the upper end of the pointer. Obviously it was extremely difficult to hold the instrument steady on the deck of a rolling ship. The Portuguese explorers of the African coast preferred, whenever possible, to take their sights ashore. They stood in towards the coast, anchored, pulled ashore, and hung their astrolabes from tripods set up on the beach. From this position they took their noon sights and worked out their latitudes with, on the whole, surprising accuracy.

For taking sights at sea the fifteenth century produced a slightly handier instrument, a rudimentary quadrant. Although lighter and simpler than the astrolabe, it worked on a similar principle and cannot have been much more accurate when the ship was rolling. Columbus on his first voyage took both an astrolabe and a quadrant with him. He used the quadrant regularly to take Pole Star sights. There is no record of his taking sun sights, or of his using the astrolabe at all. On his second voyage he seems to have left it behind.

(ii) *Ships.* At the beginning of the fifteenth century the seaborne trade of Europe was carried in ships markedly inferior in design and workmanship to the vessels used in many parts of the East; but at the end of the sixteenth century the best European ships were the best in the world. They were, perhaps, less handy and less weatherly than the junks of the China seas, but in general, in their combination of sea-worthiness, endurance, carrying capacity and fighting power they proved superior to anything else afloat, and they have retained that superiority ever since. The importance of this factor in the story of European expansion is obvious. As in their navigation, so in the design of their ships, European seafarers first borrowed and imitated, then developed and improved their borrowings beyond recognition.

Much of the trade of fifteenth-century Europe was carried in galleys. Oared vessels were preferred in the Mediterranean for their reliability and their independence of the wind. Galleys won the battle of Lepanto, as late as 1571; they did not disappear altogether until the eighteenth century; but they were obviously unsuitable for exploration or for any kind of deep-sea work, and for trade in rougher water the maritime nations of Europe had already by 1400 considerable numbers of sea-going ships which used oars only in emergency, if at all. Some of these ships were surprisingly large; they were heavy, usually clinker-built, and very broad in the beam. Their build gave them stability, and enabled their topsides to be built up to a considerable height. For purposes of war, additional height was given by fitting raised 'castles' fore and aft to accommodate cross-bowmen and the light artillery of the time, and to facilitate boarding. These castles in the Middle Ages had usually been temporary structures, and shipbuilding towns often had guilds of castle-wrights, specialized craftsmen whose trade was to convert merchantmen into men-of-war by fitting them with castles. Already by 1400, however, the practice was growing of building a permanently raised fo'c'sle and poop as part of the structure of big ships, a practice carried to extremes in the early sixteenth century.

The European ship of about 1400 was almost always square-rigged, and the limitations of square-rig accentuated the clumsiness of the hull. Unless the wind were astern or nearly so, the ship tended to make excessive leeway, and a head wind kept it in harbour. Square-rig, on the other hand, has one important advantage: it enables the total sail area of a ship to be divided into a large number of units, each of a size which can be easily handled. A square-rigged ship, therefore, can carry a very large area of canvas with safety; and square-rig proved the most satisfactory rig for big ships. In 1400, however, the principle of breaking up a ship's canvas area for ease of handling was in its infancy. A few big ships had two or even three masts; most had only one. Each mast carried a single sail laced to a great yard. Topsails, in later years the main driving sails of all big ships, were introduced after 1400 and at first were of pocket-handkerchief size.

In general, the sailing ship of Western Europe, though it had attained considerable size by 1400, was still a clumsy and primitive affair. It could carry large numbers of men or a bulky cargo for comparatively short passages with a fair wind. It was wholly unsuitable for following the windings of strange coasts, exploring estuaries, meeting the dangers of shoals, lee shores and head winds. The square-rigged ship—the *nau*—played no considerable part in the early discoveries. The Portuguese preferred a borrowed alternative, the lateen caravel—a highly individual craft which betrayed Asiatic influence in its every line. Here, too, the Arabs were their teachers.

The deep-water trade of the Indian Ocean from Suez to Malabar was in the fifteenth century almost an Arab monopoly. Taking advantage of the alternating monsoons, Arab shipmasters maintained a regular seasonal trade then, as they do to-day. The ships now engaged in the trade, especially the largest type, the Persian Gulf *baghlas,* show unmistakable European influence in the transom stern, with its elaborate carved ornament, and in the method of fastening the hull with iron spikes. In the fifteenth century all Arab ships were probably double-ended, and their planks were sewn to the frames with coir fibre. The characteristic features of design—the 'grab' bow, the deep keel, the absence of raised fo'c'sle, the long poop—are pure Arab and were much the same then as now. The hulls were carvel-built, and then as now constructed mainly of Malabar teak, a more durable material than European oak.[3]

In rig, as in hull design, the larger Arab ships have probably changed little since the fifteenth century. They have usually two masts with a pronounced forward rake. Each mast carries a single lateen sail; a triangular or nearly triangular sail, the leading edge of which is laced to a long yard hoisted obliquely to the mast. The lateen sail is the special contribution of the Arabs to the development of the world's shipping; it is as characteristic of Islam as the crescent itself. It is also a very efficient general-purpose rig. The qualities of any sail when beating to windward depend largely on its having the leading edge as long and as taut as possible; these qualities are supplied in the

---

[3] In contrast to "clinker-built" hulls, where the planking overlapped in the manner of clapboards, carvel-built hulls had the edges of the planks forming a smooth outside surface.

lateen sail by the long yard, and by simple adjustments the set of the sail can be altered to suit almost any wind conditions.

The Arab lateen rig has two serious disadvantages. One is the difficulty of going about; the yard has to be carried over the masthead, a complicated and awkward manœuvre. Under Indian Ocean wind conditions it is rarely necessary to go about; and if he must alter course, the Arab ship-master will usually wear round. The other disadvantage is more fundamental: the size and weight of the spars. The design of the lateen sail is such that only one sail can be carried on each mast. The sails must therefore be large ones, and very long spars are needed to carry them. The length of the main yard is usually about the same as the overall length of the ship. It is made of two or three lengths of teak fished together, and is naturally very heavy. Obviously there is a limit to the size of spar which can be handled, and this factor limits the size of the ship. In spite of these disadvantages, however, Arab ships in general are handy, reliable and seaworthy craft; and those used for crossing the Indian Ocean in the early fifteenth century were far better designed than any purely European type in use at the time.

The lateen-rig and Arab notions of hull design spread into the Mediterranean as a result of the Muslim incursions, and were no doubt studied and imitated by the Portuguese in the course of their long conflict with the Moors of North Africa. The Portuguese retained, however, European methods of hull construction and fastening. As a consequence, the caravels in which Prince Henry's captains made most of their voyages differed in rig and design, though not in construction, from the square-rigged ships of the rest of western Europe, and resembled in most respect the *Sambuks* which may be seen in any Red Sea harbour to-day.

Unlike the Arabs, however, the Portuguese did not rest content with the lateen-rig as they found it. The caravel did not remain a ✓constant type; it developed steadily through the fifteenth century, as long-range exploring voyagers revealed its defects. In the first place the difficulty of going about was overcome by shortening the yards, by setting them more nearly upright, and fitting them more snugly to the masts. This made it unnecessary to carry the yard over the mast-head when going about, the yard being kept always on the same side of the mast, as in modern Mediterannean lateen boats. The loss of sail area caused by these changes was compensated by stepping a mizen mast, thus giving the caravel three masts instead of two.

The number of masts could not be increased indefinitely, however, and as the Portuguese captains ventured farther and farther from home, they began to find their caravels too small for the long voyages they had to make and the stores they had to carry. We have seen that a purely lateen-rigged ship cannot be increased in size beyond a certain point without loss of efficiency, and that the Arabs never found a solution of this problem. Towards the end of the fifteenth century, the ship designers of Portugal and Spain found a solution by combining the advantages of European square-rig with those of the oriental lateen in one vessel. This vessel was the *caravela redonda,* the square-rigged caravel, employed in most voyages of discovery in the late fifteenth and early sixteenth centuries. It had a kind of primitive barquentine rig, usually with square sails on the foremast—course and topsail, and later, top-gallant also. It retained lateen-rig on main and mizen. The distribution of square and lateen sails varied to some extent; the main-mast might be squared-rigged like the fore; and sometimes there were four masts, two of them square-rigged. The square-rigged caravel retained the advantages of the lateen when sailing close-hauled, and its greater spread of canvas made it much faster when running.

The successful combination of square- and lateen-rig in one vessel was an event of the first importance in the history of European shipping. It quickly extended not only to light vessels of the caravel type, but to big ships also. By the early sixteenth century ships all over Europe were normally fitted with one or more lateen sails. The famous *Henri Grace à Dieu,* for instance, built to Henry VIII's orders, although she retained the traditional hull design with enormous castles fore and aft, was of composite rig. She had five masts, three square-rigged, the other two lateen; and though a very large ship for her day, she was a reasonably fast sailer, could sail reasonably close to the wind, and was much easier to steer than she would have been with square-rig alone.

The spread of the combined rig made possible a change in the nature of exploring voyages. The early voyages on the west coast of Africa were reconnaissances carried out by one or two caravels. The later voyages, to India and across the Atlantic, from the last decade of the fifteenth century, were made by powerful fleets including both ships and caravels, the two types being by then capable of sailing in company in all reasonable weathers; and the caravels came to be employed, to some extent, as escorts for the larger cargo-carrying ships.

It should be clear from all this that fifteenth-century Spanish and Portuguese caravels were stout, handy and seaworthy. They were not the tubs or cockle-shells of popular history, and all but the smallest were fully decked. They must, nevertheless, have been extremely uncomfortable. There was no provision of sleeping accommodation except the cabin for senior officers aft. A caravel had no raised fo'c'sle, as a rule, and the fore-peak was filled with cables and gear. There were no hammocks; those were an invention of the American Indians. The ship's company slept on the deck or the hatch-covers as best they could, and in bad weather down below. That must have been singularly unpleasant; apart from rats and cockroaches, all wooden ships leak to some extent, and pumping out seems to have been a daily routine for the morning watchmen. In bad weather there was probably no dry space in the ship. Cooking was carried out in an open fire box in the bows, the bottom of which was filled with sand. On the sand a wood fire was built when the weather allowed. Food consisted of salt beef and pork, beans, chick-peas and ship's biscuit; except, perhaps, for a short-lived supply of fresh provisions for the after-cabin. It is interesting to notice that in Lisbon there were extensive biscuit ovens belonging to the Crown and only a stone's-throw from the royal palace. Water in cask soon becomes foul, and large quantities of wine were carried, the normal daily allowance per man being about one-and-a-half litres. The wine and water casks provided the principal ballast of the ship.

Columbus's fleet on his first voyage carried ninety men, of whom perhaps forty sailed in the *Santa Maria*. Considering that she was not much bigger than a Brixham trawler, this was over-crowding by modern standards; but since she carried no soldiers she was much less over-crowded than the warships of the time. The ship's company seem to have worked a two-watch system, the watches being much the same as they are now. The master and the pilot were the two officers in charge of the two watches. At that time ships intended for sea-fighting often carried a sailing-master who worked the ship and a pilot who navigated her, as well as the captain, who commanded her. The captain was not necessarily a professional seaman; in a man-of-war he was more often a soldier. It was only with the development of naval gunnery that soldiers were ousted from sea-going command.

(iii) *Guns.* Sea-fighting in the later Middle Ages was chiefly a matter of laying alongside and boarding. Galleys were sometimes fitted with rams, but it is unlikely that they ever did much damage with them. Sailing ships designed for fighting were built up fore and aft, originally in order to give their boarding-parties the advantage of height. These superstructures proved so convenient for purposes of cabin accommodation that they remained a distinctive feature of most big ships long after the original reason for them had disappeared. In the fifteenth and sixteenth centuries the castles and fighting tops in big warships were manned by soldiers, who were carried for fighting and who were a body distinct from the sailors who worked the ship.

It is difficult to say who first introduced ship-borne artillery, and when. Probably the Venetians first used it in the fourteenth century in their incessant quarrels with the Genoese. By the middle of the fifteenth century most big European fighting ships carried guns—usually small brass pieces mounted in the castle structures fore and aft. They were intended to supplement cross-bow and arquebus fire in raking the enemy's upper deck. The Portuguese caravel, however, widely used for exploration and for escort duties in hostile seas, had no raised fo'c'sle, only a modest poop, and no fighting tops. In caravels, the guns were mounted in the bows and on the poop, and if greater fire power were required, ranged along the waist firing over the gunwale. Towards the end of the fifteenth century, embrasures were cut in the gunwales for the guns to fire through. This practice of broadside fire, once introduced, quickly spread to the great ships of all the European nations. The substitution of cast for built-up barrels also produced a type of artillery too heavy to be housed in the castle structures, and in the early sixteenth century, shipwrights hit upon the revolutionary idea of mounting guns between decks and piercing the ship's side with ports. At first these ports were small round holes allowing no traverse for the guns, so that all fire had to be point-blank; but in the course of the sixteenth century they developed into big square ports with hinged scuttles which could be secured against the sea in bad weather. The guns were then fitted with wedges for purposes of elevation and tackles for training, and continued to be so fitted until the nineteenth century.

The development of broadside fire affected not only naval tactics, but ship construction. The mounting of large numbers of guns along the ships' sides increased the top weight and the strain on the ships' timbers. The desire to counteract these tendencies, among other reasons, produced the 'tumble-home' of the sides, which became a characteristic feature of wooden warships from the sixteenth century onwards. In extreme cases, especially in big Spanish ships, the width of the upper deck was only about half the water-line width. When two such ships lay alongside one another, their gunwales were so far apart that boarding was extremely difficult; a circumstance which helped to emphasize the importance of gunnery in sea-fighting.

The Portuguese, the leaders of all Europe in nautical matters in the fifteenth century, seem to have been the first people to recognize the gun and not the foot-soldier as the main weapon in naval warfare, and to use guns against the enemy's ships rather than against his men. Significantly, the first battles fought on the principle of sinking ships by gunfire were fought in the Indian Ocean, not in the Atlantic or the Mediterranean.

NOTES

Roger C. Anderson, *The Sailing Ship: 6000 Years of History*, London, 1926.

G. S. Laird Clowes, *Sailing Ships: Their History and Development*, 2 Vols., New York, 1931–36.

Jan Hartog, *The Sailing Ship*, New York, 1964.

Björn Landström, *The Ship: An Illustrated History*, Garden City, 1961.

Michael Lewis, *The Armada Guns*, London, 1961.

Christopher Lloyd, *Ships and Seamen: From the Vikings to the Present Day*, Cleveland, 1961.

Eva G. R. Taylor, *The Haven-Finding Art*, London, 1956.

Alan Villiers (ed.), *Men, Ships and the Sea*, Washington, 1962.

THE ORIGINAL INITIATIVE— PRINCE HENRY THE NAVIGATOR *

Henry H. Hart

The most important single event in the history of exploration was the decision of a young Portuguese prince to promote the discovery of the sea route around Africa. This occurred about the time he returned from playing a prominent part in the Portuguese capture of the Moroccan port of Ceuta in 1415. His father, the king, gave him a base of operations at Sagres, on Cape St. Vincent, the southwest tip of Portugal, and provided him with funds by making him head of a military-religious order with a well-filled treasury.

If one is inclined to speculate on the ifs of history, it would be easy to argue that if Henry had not made that decision, Portugal might never have embarked upon its brilliant but exhausting pioneer work in maritime expansion. It was a relatively small country with little maritime experience beyond fishing. (The English are inclined to explain Prince Henry's initiative on the ground that his mother, Queen Philippa, was English, granddaughter of King Edward III.)

At any rate, Henry undertook the work and went at the promotion of exploration in a remarkably effective manner, considering that there

* Reprinted with permission of The Macmillan Company from *Sea Road to the Indies* by Henry H. Hart. Copyright 1950 by Henry H. Hart. (New York: The Macmillan Company, 1960, pp. 6–10.)

*were virtually no precedents. He gathered at Sagres the best records,
talents, and expert advice he could find, and soon began sending his
captains down the west coast of Africa with orders to keep going as far
as they could.*

*By the time of Henry's death in 1460, the Portuguese had rounded
Cape Verde and were exploring the Guinea Coast. The royal family
continued his policy, culminating in the voyage of Vasco da Gama
around the Cape of Good Hope to India in 1497–1499.*

The one man to whom more than to any other was due the advance-
ment of nautical science in Europe and the systematic expansion of
maritime enterprise in Portugal was the Infante Enriques, better known
to the world as Prince Henry the Navigator.

Born in 1394, Henry, the third son of King John I and Philippa of
Lancaster, daughter of John of Gaunt, as a boy had heard numberless
tales of the Moors and his people's wars with them. He had heard as
well marvelous stories of Africa—of the caravans that came up out of
the Sahara heavily laden with ivory and gold dust, ostrich plumes and
skins—and lurid accounts of wild beasts and wilder people. From early
boyhood he appears to have had his thoughts ever turned to the Dark
Continent, of which only the northern fringe was known to Europe.
Winning his spurs in 1415 as a soldier at the siege of Ceuta, in Morocco,
his experiences there aroused a deeper interest than ever in Africa.[1]
He greedily absorbed every available bit of information concerning the
routes followed by the caravans from the far interior, and learned much
from the merchants of Oran about articles of trade and the people in the
hinterland. He added to his store of knowledge the tales of traders from
Timbuktu and Gambia and the Niger country. He studied all the maps
that he could find—even though they were very crude, and more often
inaccurate than correct. He studied minutely the more scientific charts
drawn with care by the Jewish cartographers of Majorca. When finally
the expedition returned from Ceuta to Portugal, the prince resolved to
bend every effort to seek a road to the rich lands of Guinea by way of the
sea, and so to avoid dealing with the Arabs of the African Mediterranean
littoral. For the remainder of his life (with the exception of certain
political episodes with which we are not concerned here) he con-
centrated all his thoughts, efforts, and resources to the accomplishing of
this end.

[1] Another grandson of John of Gaunt, son of King Edward III of England, was
King Henry V, who won the brilliant but sterile victory of Agincourt over the
French in 1415, the same year in which Prince Henry won his spurs at Ceuta
and probably started his promotion of exploration.

Henry's motives in his enterprise were manifold, and historians have not ceased to this day their arguments and disagreements about his character or his aims. According to Henry's contemporary chronicler, Gomes Eanes Azurara, the prince had five reasons which motivated him in his project. The first was "a wish to know the land that lay beyond the Canaries and Cape Bojador, and to this he was stirred by his zeal for the service of God and of the King Edward his lord and brother who then reigned." [2] The second was to develop trade with such lands, especially Christian, "which traffic would bring great profit to our countrymen." The third was to learn as much as possible "how far the power of the infidels extended" in Africa. The fourth was the desire to find a Christian monarch who would aid Portugal in its wars against the same infidels. The fifth was to send out missionaries "to bring to him all the souls that should be saved."

Of these reasons the first was a utilitarian one—to expand and develop a knowledge of geography. The second and fourth were doubtless based on the legends and vague reports of the land of Prester John, supposedly in East Africa or Asia. The fifth reason was a desire to proselytize—for the crusading spirit was by no means dead in Portugal, and played an important part in the early Portuguese maritime enterprises.

It is a strange paradox that the prince to whom history usually refers as the Navigator hardly ever "navigated." The longest voyages that he made were probably never out of sight of land. They were between Portugal and the African coasts about Ceuta and Tangier. None the less he was the initiator of the era of great discoveries by sea.

This does not imply that Henry's ideas, plans, and enterprises were entirely original, for maps, portolanos, sailing directions, rutters, and traditions of the sea had existed from earliest times. Moreover, innumerable merchans, pilgrims, and missionaries had wandered through the Levant and much of Asia during the period of the Crusades, and later had furnished much valuable information, as well as a stimulus, to the search for a direct sea route to the rich East by way of Africa— provided there was open ocean between—a point about which there was much doubt in Europe.

Portugal was the logical point of departure for such a quest. Its

[2] Cape Bojador, the "jutting cape" on the coast of Morocco opposite the Canary Islands, was played up by the Moors as the outer limit of navigation for Europeans; beyond it, they said, there were boiling seas, sea serpents, and a sun so hot it would turn men black. This so scared the superstitious Portuguese sailors that one ship after another sent south by Henry mutinied until one bold captain finally passed it in 1434, the first major victory in the expansion movement.

harbors had been for centuries ports of call for the traffic between the Mediterranean and the coasts of the countries in the West, as well as with the British Isles. Moreover, the land itself faced the unknown, unexplored, and mysterious Atlantic.

Whether the project of finding a sea road to the Indies was uppermost or even of great importance in the mind of Prince Henry in his early enterprises is open to grave doubt. However, it seems certain that with the passing of the years it eventually became his most cherished dream and desire. Moreover, as one discovery followed another along the African coast, and as better maps were made, winds and currents more closely and carefully studied, and instruments and methods of navigation perfected, the chances of finding such a sea route became increasingly probable.

The prize promised to be worth the struggle. It meant capturing at least a large part of the wealth that was pouring into the coffers of Venice and Genoa, as well as into Moslem treasuries, for it meant obtaining both the cargoes and carrying trade of the Indies. Henry's immediate object, however, was to divert the desert trade which was enriching the Barbary despots and forcing the galleys and caravels of the Christians to seek their cargoes in infidel ports. Then, too, as he was Grand Master of the Order of Christ, the opportunity of entering new and virgin fields for the conversion of the heathen was one not to be neglected.

Henry's projects brought in their train many problems of navigation which required solution before any considerable measure of success was to be expected. The leaders of each expedition brought back charts of the coasts they visited, sailing directions, notes on landmarks for taking bearings, on winds, shoals, rocks, safe and dangerous anchorages, places where water, wood, and food might be obtained, and so on. For future and repeated voyages all these data had to be collated and systematized. This brought about careful charting of larger and larger areas and made ventures into more extensive operations safer. But the most important difficulty in the prince's undertakings was the finding of solutions of certain astronomical problems the answers to which were all-important for successful deep-sea navigation. It was in this field that Prince Henry, his collaborators, and successors were eminently successful, raising the Portuguese mariners in an incredibly short time to the position of the foremost navigators of Europe. Other merchant marines, such as those of Genoa and Venice, were indeed very important, but their voyages followed well known and constantly traveled routes, with the object of transporting Oriental goods to European ports and taking back European products to the East. The Portuguese also sailed to the

Levant, Normandy, and England, and had warehouses and agents in
Flanders. Now, however, they were to strike boldly out into unknown
seas and explore savage lands, to struggle not only against the perils of
the sea but to throw off the age-old accumulation of superstitions, the
imagined terrors and horrors of the world beyond the horizon which
had haunted mankind since its childhood.

Henry's real activities began after his Ceuta experience, though
contemporaries tell of ships dispatched by him along the African coast
as early as 1412. They recount, too, that "he always kept a number of
armed ships at sea to guard against the infidels, who then made very
great havoc upon the coasts both on this side the straits and beyond;
so that the fear of his vessels kept in security all the shores of our Spain
and the greater part of the merchants who traded between East and
West."

The better to concentrate on his plans and supervise their execution,
the prince left Lisbon and settled in or near the town of Lagos, in the
southern Algarve region of Portugal. He also established a small town
named for him "Villa do Infante," very near Cape Saint Vincent.[3]
These havens had already been visited often by vessels of many nations
passing in and out of the Strait of Gibraltar, as they were most convenient shelters and well fitted for the watering, provisioning, careening,
and repairing of ships. He employed the finest mathematicians, cartographers, and makers of nautical instruments that he could attract to
him. The most competent and famous was Jahuda Cresques (better
known as Master Jacome), a Jew.

The most difficult mathematical problem propounded to Henry and
his collaborators was fixing with certainty the position of a ship at sea
or a point on the land. The stars had been used for centuries, and after
the twelfth century the compass, brought from China probably by the
Arabs, and elaborated by them and their Christian rivals, came into
common use. Then came the cross-staff, astrolabe, and quadrant, all
of which had been developed to a high degree of efficiency by the Arabs,
who for centuries had made long voyages across the seas between Asia,
Africa, and India. These various instruments and their use were for the
most part introduced by the Jews of Spain and Portugal, who were
often the intermediaries between the Moslems and their Christian
neighbors.

As the mariners crept farther down the western coast of Africa,
they entered the findings of their instruments on their maps and in
their logbooks, so that gradually more or less reliable charts became

[3] Henry's headquarters became known as "Cape Sagres," the sacred cape.
Infante is the Portuguese word for Prince.

available to those following them. At the beginning the entries were careless and haphazard, according to the disposition and whim of the individual navigator. The notations were not accurate, nor, as King Affonso V stated in a royal letter of October 22, 1443, "were they [the lands beyond Cape Bojador] marked on sailing charts or mappe-mondes except as it pleased the men who made them." Prince Henry corrected this, and ordered that all information derived from observations of his officers be entered on their navigation charts. Proceeding carefully along these lines, the Portuguese became the founders of the modern science of cartography. Unfortunately, the original maps and instruments used before the sixteenth century have disappeared through fire, loss, carelessness, or in the great Lisbon earthquake of 1755. But the results remain.

Thus the Infante, with dogged and undaunted persistence, led his people on a quest which, before it lost its impetus, had covered the seven seas. The results of his lifetime of planning and effort, examined from the modern viewpoint—when men are equipped with every scientific device for navigation, reliable charts, swift ships not dependent on wind or current, and well provided with food and every protection for the personnel—may seem pitifully meager. But when we consider the tiny tonnage of their vessels, dependent entirely upon sails, the crudeness of their equipment, the comparative ignorance of their navigators, the pathetic inadequacy of their provisions, their ignorance of the seas they sailed and the lands they sought, the achievement of the Portuguese borders on the incredible.

VASCO DA GAMA—
AROUND AFRICA TO INDIA *

Henry H. Hart

The second of the great voyages of exploration carried Henry the Navigator's project through to completion. In 1497 the king of Portugal sent Vasco da Gama out around the southern tip of Africa to India. Already in 1488 Bartholomeu Dias had reached that tip; he named

* Reprinted with permission of The Macmillan Company from *Sea Road to the Indies* by Henry H. Hart. Copyright 1950 by Henry H. Hart. (New York: The Macmillan Company, 1960, pp. 121-129, 132-133, 154-157.)

*it the Stormy Cape, but the king changed this to the Cape of Good
Hope, because the way to India at last seemed clear. But neither Dias
nor anyone else was sent out immediately to verify this; instead nine
years elapsed before da Gama was finally picked for the mission. In the
meantime Columbus had completed two voyages to America.*

*The first important feature of da Gama's voyage, described in the
following passage, was his navigating skill in developing a new sea
route to Good Hope. Instead of hugging the west coast of Africa with
its baffling winds, he struck across the South Atlantic almost to Brazil
before doubling back on a southeastward course in order to take advantage of the prevailing winds. From that time on, down through the
whole age of sail, that new course was followed.*

*Around Good Hope da Gama had a mutiny to quell, and then
encountered the hostility of some of the Arabs established in the ports of
East Africa. But at one of these, Malindi, the ruler was friendly and
loaned da Gama a skillful pilot who navigated him to his destination,
the port of Calicut on the Malabar Coast of western India. It was one
of the richest entrepots for the spices of Southeast Asia; the Arabs
purchased them for shipment by way of the Persian Gulf or Red Sea
and then overland to the Mediterranean, where they were picked up by
the Italians from Venice or Genoa. The Arab traders at Calicut realized
the threat to this long-standing, highly profitable Arab-Italian trade, if
the Portuguese were able to develop an all-water route to Lisbon, which
would eliminate transshipments and middlemen's profits. Consequently
they did all they could to obstruct da Gama and his men, who barely
escaped with a cargo of spices, when things became rough. His little
squadron, battered and with only a fraction of its original force, finally
reached Lisbon in 1499; and the Portuguese went wild with celebration.
They were on the threshold of an ambitious century in the East,
though it was to prove an exhausting one.*

*In comparison with Columbus' first voyage, da Gama's offers some
interesting contrasts. So far as initiative went, Columbus stood far
ahead. He had determined to sail westward into the Atlantic and had had
a long, frustrating experience before finding someone to finance his
experiment. Da Gama, on the other hand, had suddenly been selected
as a rather passive agent of a policy that the Portuguese royal family
had been pursuing for more than 80 years. As a navigator da Gama's
development of the new South Atlantic route was brilliant; and he was
out of sight of land much longer than Columbus. Da Gama's voyage
led to more immediate profitable trade for the Portuguese than the
Spaniards developed in America. Columbus was sailing into the unknown, whereas da Gama knew before he started what he would find*

at the far end, because the King of Portugal had sent out a scout to report on Calicut. Incidentally, in their overseas dealings da Gama was often too brutal and Columbus not tough enough.

The great adventure was at hand. All difficulties had been surmounted, all delays were at an end, the day of sailing had been determined, and all that remained were the last farewells of the mariners to their families and the commending of themselves to God's care during the hazardous voyage.

About four miles west of the Arsenal of Lisbon the river Tagus widened for a space, providing ample anchorage for a fleet in midstream. There was located the suburb of Restello, on the right bank of the river, where the blue waters gently lapped a beach of golden sand. On the long slope between shore and hills lay broad orchards and green gardens, and here and there on the heights the dark sails of windmills turned merrily in the brisk ocean breezes. The south bank of the river was steep and wooded, and deep ravines came down to the water's edge.

Here the ships of Gama's fleet, new, shining, and freshly painted, with flags and pennons flying bravely in the wind, had dropped anchor opposite a little chapel on the shore. It had been built many years before by Prince Henry the Navigator and was dedicated by him to St. Mary of Bethlehem. There the crews of departing ships were wont to offer up their prayers and petitions for a prosperous voyage and a safe return. On the evening of July 7, 1497, Vasco da Gama rode down from Lisbon to the little church and there kept vigil the whole night long with his brother Paulo, his other officers, and the priests of the near-by monastery of Santo Thomar, making confession of his sins and praying for strength and success.

Soon after sunrise on July 8, men and women began to gather about the chapel, until the shore was crowded. The sailors were there from the fleet, sun-bronzed, barefooted, in loose trousers, tight cotton shirts, and red caps. With them were the men-at-arms in gorget, breastplate, and helmet. All were surrounded by their families and friends. Many of the womenfolk, even though in bright-colored garments, wore black mantles over their heads and shoulders and appeared more like mourners at a funeral than those come to bid a cheering farewell to a ship's company of young and lusty men bound for high adventure. Presently (according to the quaint account of the chronicler Osorio), as though by a common impulse, they gave vent to their emotions in loud cries and lamentations. They burst into tears, crying:

Ah miserable mortals! See to what a fate such ambition and greed are rushing you headlong! What more dreadful punishments could be visited upon you if you had committed the most heinous of crimes? What far distant and measureless seas you must penetrate, what merciless and mountainous waves you must brave, and what dangers threaten your very lives in those faraway lands! Would it not be wiser for you to face death in whatsoever fashion [it may come] here at home than to launch forth into hidden places far from your fatherland, and to find graves in the salt depths of the sea?

Whether or not this opera-chorus lament was really heard on Tagus's banks that day we shall never know, but we can be sure that similar sentiments filled the hearts of many at that moment. We are told that Gama himself shed tears, austere and severely self-disciplined as he was. He brushed them aside hastily, however, and gathering together his officers and crew, led the way into the chapel for the final Mass.

The building was too small to admit all who desired to participate, and many of the crew with their families and friends were forced to stand outside in the sun, bareheaded, throughout the solemn ceremony. The scene within was a vivid and colorful one. The small windows admitted but little of the sunlight, and in the gloom the candles and tapers gleamed on gold and silver and steel and jewels, accenting helmet and sword hilt and breastplate, and glowed dully on the velvet of cloaks and the silk of consecrated flags. When the closing words of the Mass had been intoned, the bells of the chapel and the monastery were rung. Immediately a procession was formed from the church to the shoreline, where the ship's boats had been drawn up on the sand. The vicar of the chapel led the way, followed by the priests and friars with folded hands and bowed heads, walking slowly and solemnly, chanting a litany as they went. They were followed by acolytes swinging smoking censers, and behind came the cross-bearer and more chanting priests in their long robes. Next came Gama, alone, head erect, severe and unsmiling, looking neither to the right nor to the left, and bearing a lighted candle. Behind him the officers and crew of the fleet fell into line two by two, each man likewise carrying a lighted candle. And so, with blue clouds of incense, the measured chanting of the litany, and the murmur of the responses from the multitude, the long procession reached the foreshore. The vicar turned, and at a sign all present knelt with bowed heads. The priest held a general confession and granted plenary absolution for their sins to all who might lose their lives in the venture. The multitude arose as the religious service ended, and at an order from the captains the officers and men entered their boats and rowed off to their vessels.

The river Tagus presented a brave sight that far-off July day, crowded as it was with boats filled with men in shining armor, or clad in crimson and green, yellow and white, blue and purple. Flags and pennons of every shape, size, and color fluttered in the breeze, the motley livery of servingmen and the crowds on shore in their bright garments, together with the silvery flash of rising and falling oars added to the brilliant tapestry of the scene. It was a sight to stir one's heart, for, as one old chronicler has it, "it appeared in no way like the sea, but like unto a field of flowers."

Marshaled on deck, the assembled men-at-arms blew a loud fanfare on their trumpets. As the royal standard was hoisted to the masthead of the *São Gabriel,* the musicians beat out a great bass ruffle on their kettledrums; and the pipes and timbrels, flutes and tambours added to the din, drowning out the groans and cries and lamentations of those left behind on shore or in the small boats in which many had rowed out to catch a last glimpse of their dear ones aboard the ships.

And now it was afternoon, and, as usual at that season, as the shadows grew longer a keen wind arose and blew down the river toward the sea. The admiral had planned to take advantage of this wind and he gave the order to weigh anchor. The men jumped to the task with a will, in an effort to forget the trying hours behind them, when they had torn themselves away from grieving parents, families, or sweethearts. The anchors slowly and grudgingly rose dripping from the river's mud to the rousing rhythm of on old sea chantey. The next order was to set the sails. As the crew heaved and hauled, the wind caught the canvas and bellied it out, revealing on each sail the great painted red cross of the Order of Christ, the same cross as that emblazoned on the flag that Manuel had entrusted to Gama a few days previously at Montemór o Novo. The ships felt the first strength of the wind—that wind which was to be their servant (but too often a raging, rebellious, and sullen servant) for many, many thousands of weary miles—and, obedient to the helm, heeled slightly over and slowly gained headway down the river.

People still lined the shore, straining their eyes to catch hoped-for recognitions. Hands were waved, scarfs were shaken in the wind, and cries and shouts came faintly over the water to the ships as they dropped down toward the sea on tide and wind. The men crowded to the bulwarks and swarmed up the rigging, while officers leaned on the poop rail and out the sterncastle windows, all eager for one last sight of the crowds, of their beloved city of Lisbon with its hills and valleys, palaces and churches, now gradually dropping astern. The long rays of the setting sun gleamed on spearhead and cannon, ship's gear and helmet, and on shore it touched with flaming red-gold the stone and scaffolding of the half-completed Cathedral of the Sea. They gleamed once more on the waters of the Tagus, now turned a burnished steel-gray. Then twilight descended.

With the coming of the dusk the crowds on shore gradually dispersed and returned in small groups to their homes. The wind freshened as the fleet drew nearer the open sea. In the dim twilight a few fishing boats with rust-colored sails hastily scudded out of the path of the high ships bearing down on them. Flags were hauled down and stowed in their lockers, the night watches were set, lanterns were hauled aloft, and night fell on land and ships and river. The greatest adventure of the Portuguese nation had begun, the final realization of the dreams of Prince Henry and the plans and labors of King John II. It had taken the best part of a century to bring these dreams and plans to fruition—years of travail and disappointment, of trial and error, of success and failure. It had cost the lives of many brave men and also much gold. But Manuel, called by history the Fortunate, was to become the richest monarch in Europe; while Portugal was for a time to rule over many far-off lands and seas and peoples never before under European dominion, and for the greater part unknown, except for the tales of Marco Polo and a few other daring souls.

Few aboard the ships slept that night. Hearts were too full and excitement burned too high. But with the coming of a new day, all were early astir and active. They had crossed the bar, no land was in sight, and they were alone with sea and sky and God, their only company that of the squawking, quarreling white and gray gulls that followed the ships on their voyage far out into the western ocean.

As the crew of the *São Gabriel* went about their usual tasks, they had their first opportunity of seeing their commander at close range. They beheld, above them on the poop deck, a man in a beretlike velvet cap. He was medium of stature, in the full manhood of his thirty-odd years, rather thick-set, with face and neck the dark brick-red of one long exposed to tempest and hot sun and the salt of the sea. His features were partially covered by a black mustache and a full spade beard; but these rather accentuated than hid the strength of square jaw, the full and sensual, yet firm, even hard, mouth. His eyes were quick, keen, and wary, surrounded by the tiny network of wrinkles of one who had faced sun and wind and the glare of the sea for long years. At times there was revealed in the quickly veiled eyes and compressed lips a latent cruelty, seemingly an innate part of his nature. He was not a man to be loved, or one who courted affection. But the hard-bitten sailors, who had sailed the African seas with such men before, saw in him a man of iron will and inflexibility of purpose. They recognized in his voice, his quick, decisive orders, his whole appearance and bearing, a competent mariner, a stern disciplinarian, and a man not to be crossed or challenged. They knew he had the full confidence of the king, and that, come what might, he would execute his sovereign's will to the letter. Withal, they knew him from reputation as a brave man, and one who would never hesitate to lead wherever he ordered others to go. Those who were fortunate enough to return with Gama to Lisbon, and who fared forth with him again to the Indies, were to see all that was written on their admiral's face translated often into swift action—the determination, the intelligence, the stubbornness, the unreasoning, terrible anger, and the cold-blooded cruelty that was nothing short of sadistic. He was to bring victory and undreamed-of riches to King Manuel, and he was to lay the seas and lands of the Indies at his feet; but he was also to bring unnecessary suffering and horrible torture and death in almost unbelievably fiendish forms to untold numbers of unhappy folk, whose only sin was that they were not of Gama's faith, and whose only crime was that they had unwittingly crossed his path as he relentlessly pursued his star.

And so the fateful expedition set sail; and in the words of the author of the *Roteiro* of Vasco da Gama's first voyage to India, "we departed from Restello on a Saturday, which was the eighth day of July of the said year 1497, on our voyage, [and] may God Our Lord grant that we accomplish it in his service. Amen." [1]

The voyage began quietly, with no unusual or noteworthy incidents. After a run of a week to the southwest, the Canaries were sighted, and thence the ships continued on their way close to the African coast. The men cast their lines here and caught fish for their messes. Proceeding farther, the fleet ran into a dense fog on the night of the 16th, off the inlet known as the Río de Oro (River of Gold). When the sun rose on July 17, the ships had become separated in the fog and in a wind which had arisen in the night. Gama had foreseen such a contingency, and, following his orders, the ships set their course for the Cape Verde Islands. On the morning of July 22 lookout of the *São Rafael* sighted three ships off Ilha do Sal, the northeastern part of the Cape Verde groups. They were the *Berrio,* the storeship, and the vessel commanded by Bartholomeu Dias, discoverer of the Cape of Good Hope.[2] The four vessels joined company and on the evening of July 26 finally overtook the *São Gabriel.* The following day the entire fleet dropped anchor in

[1] The Roteiro, like the rutters of other nations, were the detailed, confidential navigational records.

[2] Dias, as already noted, had nine years earlier rounded the tip of Africa, which he had called the Stormy Cape but which the King had changed to Cape of Good Hope. For some reason, he was not sent right back to follow up his discovery, and he accompanied the da Gama expedition in a subordinate role.

Porto da Praia, the harbor of Santiago, largest of the Cape Verde
Islands. There the men were granted shore leave; and while repairs
were being made to the yards of the ships, stores of fresh meat, water,
and wood were taken aboard.

From the Cape Verdes a course was set to the eastward along the
Guinea Coast and Sierra Leone. After further repairs were made on
the yards of Gama's ship (probably the damage was the result of a
storm), the course was changed. Instead of keeping close to the land
in order to cover the 3,370 miles to the Cape of Good Hope, Gama
struck boldly out from the Sierra Leone coast toward the west and
south, making a great circular swing toward the hitherto undiscovered
coast of Brazil.[3] Several explanations are given for his action. One is
that he had obtained information as to the prevailing winds (and
perhaps as to land to the west) from earlier navigators; the second is
that the admiral took counsel with his officers and pilots, with the
resultant consensus that they would avoid contrary and dangerous
coastal winds by striking west. The third explanation is that Vasco da
Gama took the action on his own initiative and that "it was," in the words
of one commentator, "an act of superlative audacity." It may well be that
all three explanations are correct—that he had some information from
earlier mariners, that his officers contributed ideas and theories, and
that he himself decided to make the trial. Another possibility is that
the whole route was planned and the details were worked out before
the ships had crossed the Tagus bar.

The fact remains that in this first voyage to the East Vasco da Gama
not only opened the sea road to the Indies for his royal master, but
that he either found by chance or plotted the best sailing route from
Europe to the Cape of Good Hope, the route still used by sailing vessels
and the one advised in both the latest sailing directions of the British
Admiralty and those of the United States Hydrographic Office. The
great circular course by which he turned southwestward from Africa to
a point about 5° N. latitude, sailed to within a short (undetermined)
distance of the Brazilian coast, and swung east by southeast again at a
point approximately 20° S. latitude, gave him the advantage of the
most favorable winds and currents.

It was a long, wearisome voyage, one beset with tempests inter-
spersed with calms, and which revealed no island or coast where ships
could take on fresh water or renew their provisions and supplies of
wood.

After many days of sailing toward the southeast, whales and seals

[3] Brazil would actually be reached by Cabral on the next voyage to India, but
there have been persistent rumors that some Portuguese had already been there.

were seen on October 27, and coastal seaweed and other indications of the proximity of land were observed. Soundings were taken at intervals, and on the morning of November 1 land was sighted. The ships were signaled to draw closer together, salutes were fired, and the ships were decked out with flags to celebrate a safe arrival at the African coast after more than three months of storm and calm in mid-Atlantic. The landfall could not be identified by D'Alenquer, who, it will be remembered, had sailed along this coast with Bartholomeu Dias, so the order was given to stand out to sea and proceed farther southward. Three days later the ships again approached land and entered a broad bay where Gama sent men in a small boat to make soundings and to search for a safe anchorage. On receiving a favorable report, he sailed in with his ships and dropped anchor. The inlet was forthwith christened Santa Helena Bay, and preparations were made to clean the ships both inside and outside, to mend the sails, and in general to repair the damages suffered at sea. The supply of drinking water had run very low, and what remained was stale and foul. Men were sent out to search for fresh water and located a stream flowing into the bay four leagues from the anchorage. Following the usual custom, the stream was named the Santiago.[4]

Gama was not satisfied with the shipboard readings of the sun's altitude, for with the imperfect instruments at his command the findings made on tossing, pitching vessels could not be trusted. So, while the crews were busy with repairs, wood gathering, and the filling of the water casks, he landed to make more accurate calculations. A tripod was set up on shore, the instruments were landed, and new observations were made. As he was thus engaged, some of the crew who had wandered away from the shore and back of the sand dunes came to report that they had seen two negroes near by, little fellows who appeared to be gathering something from the ground. This pleased Gama, for he was most anxious to obtain information about the unknown coast to which they had come. He ordered his men to surround the natives silently, close in, and seize them. The natives were clothed only in sheaths of wood or leather, with which they covered their nakedness, and carried fish spears of wood tipped with horn hardened in the fire. . . . Gama, disappointed at learning nothing of the land where he was, ordered sail set two days later, on November 14. Luckily, the ship's repairs had been completed and ample stores of wood and fresh water were aboard. . . .

Gama was now in a quandary. He believed that he was in the proximity of the Cape of Good Hope but was not sure how far away

[4] Now the Berg River in South-West Africa.

he was. He looked to D'Alenquer, who had sailed these seas with Dias, but he could not help much, though his guess was within three leagues of the correct distance. So Gama made the decision himself—for indecision was never one of his faults. The course was set south-southwest. At the end of the second day the lookout shouted, "Land in sight on the port bow"; and there, in view of all, rose the welcome sight of the Cape itself, the landmark toward which Gama and his ships had been striving for almost five months. Though the Cape was before them, adverse winds prevented them from doubling it until noon of November 22, when the ships rounded the point and sailed farther along the coast, passing close to False Bay on their way.

This part of the voyage had been a severe test of Vasco da Gama's abilities as a master mariner dealing with unknown winds and currents and in weathering the sudden violent storms of the South Atlantic. He stood the test well and won the respect, admiration, and confidence of his officers and crew not only as a seaman but also as a leader of infinite resourcefulness in the handling of ships and men.[5]

.   .   .   .

Vasco da Gama was most fortunate in the choice of the pilot thus sent him by the sheik of Malindi—a pilot described as "the highest exponent of Moslem nautical science." He is referred to by the author of the *Roteiro* as "a Christian of Gujerat" and by comtemporary chroniclers as "Malémo Caná." Neither of these statements is correct. It has been conclusively established that the pilot was an Arab of Julfar, named Ahmad ibn Majid. "Malémo Caná" was the Portuguese transliteration of his Arabic title. "Mu'allim" means "the instructor, pilot, or sailing-master." "Caná" is a corruption of the Tamil "Kanagan," "an arithmetician, or a master of astronomical navigation." The son and grandson of pilots, he was a hadji, that is, a man who had made the pilgrimage to Mecca, and he had the right to wear the green turban. In *Al Muhit* (all-embracing), a book of the period treating of the navigation and nautical lore of the Indian Ocean by Sidi Ali ibn Husayn, the author, a Turkish admiral, refers to Ahmad as "the most trustworthy of the many pilots and mariners of the west coast of India in the fifteenth and sixteenth centuries—may Allah grant him mercy!" Not only was Ahmad a successful practical pilot, but he was the author of many rutters, or logbooks. Of these the manuscripts of nineteen are still in existence.

[5] Gama proceeded up the southeast coast, suppressing a mutiny, which Dias had failed to do in that stormy area. He continued on northward to Mozambique and then on to other regions held by the Arabs, who maintained trade relations with India with dhows that came and went with the seasonal monsoons. He encountered hostility and suspicion at Mombasa and elsewhere, but was well received at Malindi, which was hostile to Mombasa (both now in Kenya).

They were written between 1460 and 1495 and are remarkably full and accurate in their descriptions, especially of the monsoons and other winds of the regions traversed. Ahmad was no longer a young man when he entered Gama's employ. Born somewhere between 1430 and 1435, he was well in his sixties when Vasco da Gama arrived at Malindi.

As soon as Ahmad ibn Majid arrived on board the *São Gabriel*, the commander in chief invited him, together with the interpreter, to his cabin to become acquainted and to estimate his abilities. Ahmad unrolled his maps of the west coast of India, accurately drawn with bearings, parallels, and meridians laid down in the Arab fashion, and explained them to the commander. During the discussion the latter brought out the great wooden astrolabe which the *São Gabriel* carried, as well as the smaller brass ones which he used for taking readings of the sun. The Arab showed a perfect familiarity with these, and indicated that they and similar instruments were used by Red Sea pilots for solar and sidereal readings. He then explained the way he and other pilots of the Indian seas took their readings by *taboas*, or plates with perforations for sighting, and also elucidated the mysteries of the cross-staff. As a result of the interview Gama was convinced that he had obtained a master navigator. The outcome proved that his confidence was not misplaced.

Nothing now remained to detain Gama and his fleet any longer in Malindi. Thanks to the friendship of the sheik, the water butts were filled, the provision rooms stacked high, and a plentiful supply of wood laid in, and the generous gifts of fresh fruit and vegetables had restored the surviving members of the crew to health. The long-hoped-for pilot was aboard. The monsoon had set in. Gama gave the order to weigh anchor and set sail. On April 24 the steersman swung the prows of the ships to the northeast, the monsoon caught the sails with their great red crosses and bellied them out, and the fleet of Dom Manuel was off on the last stage of its momentous voyage to the coast of India.

The voyage from Malindi across the Indian Ocean was uneventful. Five days after leaving the coast city the Portuguese "rejoiced at seeing once more the Great and Little Bear, Orion, and the other stars about the Northern Pole." For twenty-three days the ships held steadily on their way, with the favoring monsoon ever carrying them nearer their goal. Land was sighted dimly through the haze on the twenty-third day, whereupon the pilot changed the course away from the coast. Heavy rain and a thunderstorn prevented Ahmad from identifying his position until May 20, when high land was sighted—Kotta Point. The pilot made his way to Gama, who, with his men, stood looking anxiously from the prow out over the blue waters of South India.

"We have arrived; we are just north of Calicut! Here is the land where you desired to go."

The long outward voyage was over. The thousands of weary miles of ocean, the eleven months of storm and calm, of stale food and foul water, of unfriendly savages and still more hostile Arabs lay behind them. Many of their companions, victims of scurvy and storm, of infection and fever, lay in the deep waters of the Atlantic or were in scattered graves along the African coast. But they, the survivors, had successfully won their way to the golden lands of the East, the lands of which Prince Henry and King John had dreamed, and which Bartholomeu Dias had almost reached. The sea road to India was no longer a vision of the future—it was a reality, traversed and duly charted by the indomitable commander Vasco da Gama.

He had won an enviable place in history. But the adventure of Vasco da Gama had hardly begun. He was yet to experience much on land and on sea, at home and in India. It is a pity that his fame was to be marred and besmirched by his constant lack of diplomacy, his ungovernable temper, his ruthless determination and his callous cruelty. Too many ugly pages were to be written in his story, pages which were to obscure and tarnish the glory of the great achievement, brought to a climax that hot sunny day in May, 1498, when Gama anchored off the coast of Malabar, a few miles from the famous city of Calicut.[6]

THE VOYAGES OF COLUMBUS *

Boies Penrose

If the decision of Henry the Navigator was the most important single event in the history of exploration, the first voyage of Christopher Columbus in 1492 was the most important single exploring venture.

---

* Reprinted by permission of the publishers from Boies Penrose, *Travel and Discovery in the Renaissance, 1420–1620,* Cambridge, Mass.: Harvard University Press, Copyright 1952, 1955, by the President and Fellows of Harvard College. Chap. 5, pp. 77–92.

[6] Calicut (not to be confused with Calcutta in the northeast of India) was one of the virtually independent city-states that had grown rich as entrepots in the spice trade. It had been reported upon by Covilhan, recently sent out by the Portuguese king to look things over. The attitude of the local ruler was so hostile to Gama and other Portuguese that he would be punished severely, while Goa, in that same Malabar area, would become the center of their eastern empire.

The Portuguese already knew about India at the far end of Vasco da Gama's run, but probably no one knew of the existence of America, though some argue that the Portuguese had reached it and were suppressing the news because of emphasis on the Good Hope run. In another respect Columbus differed from da Gama. The Portuguese was selected to carry out a policy sponsored by the royal family for more than 80 years; Columbus was "on his own" in trying to find a financial backer for the idea (which was by no means rare in his day) that the world was round and that the Orient could be reached more easily by crossing the Atlantic than by going around Africa. His error lay in underestimating the distance—degrees of longitude were wider than he thought. He believed that he had reached the "Indies," and his error is perpetuated in our still calling the natives Indians and the Caribbean islands the West Indies.

For the sake of his later reputation, Columbus lived too long. After he first found America, which was a superlative achievement, the rest of his career was an anticlimax. In particular, he was not sufficiently hard-boiled to be a successful colonial administrator, and his later voyages did not measure up to the first one.

As the second half of the fifteenth century wore on, discovery was more and more in the air; the quest for the Indies inspired men throughout Europe, and Portugal's powerful neighbor entered the lists, to embark on a career of exploration and conquest which was destined to have even greater consequences in the stream of world history than the epic exploits of the Portuguese. Spain had hitherto taken little part in overseas expansion, but she was not wholly without nautical experience and had in fact at least a modicum of maritime tradition behind her. Those harbors between Gibraltar and the Portuguese frontier face the Barbary Coast and the Atlantic Islands; they look southwestward across what the early chroniclers called the Ocean Sea. A hardy seafaring population grew up in these parts of Andalusia, men who at first indulged in local coasting and fishing, later voyaged to the Canary Islands, and conducted a number of expeditions to Guinea, especially during the so-called War of the Castilian Succession (1475–1480). In this sense the first Columbian voyage was by no means a novel or an isolated venture, but rather a further achievement, stemming from the West African navigation of experienced and adventurous men, who were at home on the sea. Columbus therefore was not involving himself with a nation wholly amateurish when he sought to interest the Spanish crown in a trans-Atlantic course to China; he was on the contrary associating himself with a people who had fished and traded along the coasts between the Bay of Biscay and the Gulf of Guinea.

So it was that circumstances were fortuitous; Spain had sailors and, in Andalusia at least, some experience of the sea, while Columbus had a vision and intense enthusiasm. How long Columbus had the vision no one knows, but in 1474 the future discoverer, a young man of twenty-three still living in his native Genoa, began a very serious correspondence (once questioned, but now generally accepted accepted as genuine) with Paolo Toscanelli about the possibility of reaching the Orient by a westward passage. Toscanelli was a celebrated Florentine scholar whose profession was medicine and whose hobby was geography; he admired Marco Polo in particular and accepted his theory that the Asiatic land mass extended much farther to the eastward than even Ptolemy had argued. At the same time Toscanelli held with the Ptolemaic measurement of the Earth, which gave the circumference as eighteen thousand geographical miles. This resulted in the figure of a mere five thousand miles between the Canaries and Kinsay (Hangchow)—which Columbus, with hopeful enthusiasm, further reduced to thirty-five hundred miles. Obviously then, Toscanelli would be a hearty exponent of the western route to the Indies, and his conviction was not lost on his young disciple, whose ideas, too, were fundamentally Ptolemaic and who was strongly influenced by the *Imago Mundi* of Pierre d'Ailly, to say nothing of Marco Polo and Sir John Mandeville. This curious medievalism in Columbus' thought was balanced by the practical side of his nature. such as his superb skill as a navigator; but these two sides of his character must always make him a problem for the psychologist and a puzzle for the historian.

To sum up, Columbus believed the world to be a sphere; he greatly underestimated its size; and he overestimated the extent of the Asiatic continent—concluding that the further Asia extended eastward, the nearer it came to Spain. His plan, early determined on and adhered to with unshakable tenacity, assumed that between the Azores and the eastern shores of Asia there were no lands to be discovered, and accordingly that there was no other course except to cross the Atlantic Ocean by as direct a route as possible. This perfectly reasonable forecast, and the firmness with which he held to the plans based on it rank among the most conspicuous indications of Columbus' greatness.

His experience as a sailor dated for the most part from his earlier years. As a young Genoese he had gone on one or more trading voyages in the Mediterranean, probably getting as far afield as the Greek Archipelago. In 1476 he had embarked on an enterprise for England, but the fleet was set upon by a hostile Franco-Portuguese armada off

Lagos, and the future discoverer of the New World made his landing in Portugal by swimming ashore after his ship had gone down. Because of this accident he passed into Portuguese service, and late in the same year he took part in a voyage to the British Isles and quite possibly to Iceland. (The latter venture is by no means unlikely, inasmuch as there is known to have been a lively trade between Iceland and such ports as Bristol and Galway in the later Middle Ages.) The last of these early voyages, and the one which made the most lasting impression on Columbus, was an expedition to Elmina on the Guinea coast in 1482 or the following year, in which he obviously served in a responsible capacity; moreover, sailing with skilled Portuguese pilots down the West African coast must have greatly improved his seamanship.[1] Another influence on Columbus' vision must have been his residence during most of these years in Madeira and nearby Porto Santo; he had gone to the islands about 1479 as a result of his marriage to Felipa Perestrello, the sister of the captain of Porto Santo, and until his wife's death about five years later his headquarters were in the romantic archipelago which in effect pointed the way westward into the unknown.

After his African voyage Columbus gave himself entirely to "the enterprise of the Indies," and devoted the better part of a decade in studying the problem, in planning, and in attempting to secure the backing of a royal patron. To convince rulers of his mission in life was not easy; he first tried King John II of Portugal, but that sovereign thought him (according to Barros) "a big talker, and boastful in setting forth his accomplishments, and full of fancy and imagination with his Isle Cypango [Japan], than certain whereof he spoke." Yet John was fair enough to appoint a commission to examine Columbus' proposals, and it was largely because Columbus' price was so high that negotiations fell through. In 1485 Columbus went to Spain to lay his schemes before Ferdinand and Isabella; and to have more strings to his bow, he sent his brother Bartholomew to France and England in a vain attempt to interest Charles VIII and Henry VII in outfitting a westward expedition to Cathay. Columbus' dealings with the Spanish Court were unbelievably tedious and tantalizing. It was touch-and-go almost to the last minute, and only the loyal backing of the queen made Columbus' voyage possible. Thus Christopher Columbus, after five long years of dancing attendance at court as a poor suitor while the Royal Commission examined his project, was empowered by Queen Isabella to equip a fleet which was destined to revolutionize the course of history. Reasons

[1] Columbus is said to have been present at the building of the prefabricated Portuguese fort at Elmina (The Mine) on the Gold Coast; it remained the chief Portuguese stronghold until finally captured by the Dutch.

for this delay are not far to seek; Spain was engaged in unifying herself
and in expelling the Moors—it was, as Professor Morison says, as if a
polar explorer had tried to interest Abraham Lincoln in the conquest of
the Antarctic about the time of the Battle of Gettysburg. And yet in a
larger sense, the conquest of America can be viewed as a continuation
of the *reconquista* of Spain, as a fresh adventure of expanding dominion
and crusading zeal—as well as of lucrative enterprise. To her everlasting
credit, Queen Isabella viewed the project in this broader light.[2]

First Voyage

Armed with the royal mandate, Columbus proceeded in the spring
of 1492 to Palos, a small port on the Rio Tinto near Huelva, which was
to be his base. This choice proved a happy one; Palos had an active part
in the Guinea voyages, and its shipping was largely controlled by a
family of shipowners and sea captains named Pinzon. Columbus won
over the head of the family, Martin Alonso, to his project, and the latter,
by engaging crews and procuring caravels, put the enterprise fairly on
its feet. Three vessels were chartered for the voyage: the lateen-rigged
Niña of approximately sixty tons; the square-rigged *Pinta* of about the
same size; and the flagship *Santa Maria*, a square-rigger classed as a
small ship or *nao*, rather than a caravel, and with perhaps twice the
tonnage of either of her smaller consorts. On the *Santa Maria*, Columbus
was captain, Juan de la Cosa (not to be confused with the cartographer
of the same name) was master and owner, and Peralonso Niño was pilot;
on the *Pinta*, Martin Alonso Pinzon was captain and Francisco Pinzon
master; on the *Niña*, Vincente Yañez Pinzon was captain, and Juan
Niño, pilot and owner. All these men were sailors of skill and experience,
and at least two of them (Peralonso Niño and V. Y. Pinzon) later
undertook important voyages on their own account.

At dawn on August 3, 1492, the little fleet left Palos on what was
the most important single voyage on record. Columbus had hoped to
reach the Canary Islands as his first port of call, but three days out the
Pinta's rudder broke, and the other two vessels proceeded to Gomera
alone, arriving on August 12. A delay of three weeks or more ensued,
during which the missing *Pinta* was found at Las Palmas and her rudder
repaired, and the lateen rig of the *Niña* was changed to a square rig.
On September 6 the ships set out westward into the tractless wastes of
the Atlantic. The weather was fine, the wind was favorable, and the

[2] The Moors had invaded and overrun much of Spain in 711; the Christians,
driven back into the mountains, fought them for centuries. The final Moorish
stronghold, Granada, fell in 1492, at the very time Columbus was setting out.

morale was generally high. For perhaps half the voyage Columbus clung to the twenty-eighth parallel as if he were a tight-rope walker; after that he gradually made his southing. After a month of very fast sailing, signs of land became evident, and at two in the morning on October 12 Rodrigo da Triana, on lookout on the *Pinta's* forecastle, shouted "Tierra! Tierra!"—the New World had been sighted. This land turned out to be San Salvador or Watling's Island in the Bahamas, a coral island about thirteen miles long and six across, which had a picturesque and volatile native population.[3] Columbus spent three days there, and then steered southward through the archipelago; he anchored at Rum Cay, explored Long Island, and spent four days at Crooked Island. From the friendly natives he learned of a rich and beautiful land to the south; hopeful that this was the land of the Grand Khan, he hastened southward and sighted the Cuban mountains on October 27. For the next five weeks or more he explored the northeastern coast of Cuba. His first anchorage was at Bahia Bariay; the following day he coasted westward to Puerto Padre, some forty miles, and then retraced his course as far as Puerto Gibara. At this anchorage he remained eleven days, even sending an embassy upcountry to find the Grand Khan. Futile as this mission was, his stay was not without one highly important result—it initiated Europeans into the craft and mystery of tobacco smoking. From Puerto Gibara the fleet coasted eastward and the admiral employed himself in taking various lunar and stellar observations.

All was not well in the discipline of the higher officers, however, and on November 22 Martin Alonso Pinzon sailed away in the *Pinta* without even a by-your-leave from his commander. Columbus, thoroughly exasperated by this defection, put in with the two remaining vessels at the present site of Baracoa; the weather was bad and he was detained there for a week. Native information told him of a great island to the eastward, so he made sail on December 4, and two days later sighted the northwestern tip of Hispaniola.[4] Another spell of bad weather held him a week at Moustique Bay, but he employed his time by sending an exploring party into the interior, and he took formal possession of the island for Ferdinand and Isabella. Amid a tiresome beat to windward Columbus took the fleet slowly along the northern coast, but off Cap Haitien a major disaster befell the expedition: the *Santa Maria* was wrecked on a coral reef on Christmas Day. This misfortune led to a radical change of plans. Only one ship now remained, the *Niña*, and

[3] It has been argued in recent years that Columbus's San Salvador was Caicos Island, nearer Cuba, rather than Watling's Island.
[4] The great island of Hispaniola today contains the Republic of Haiti on the end nearer Cuba and the Dominican Republic on the end nearer Puerto Rico.

she was too small to take her consort's crew back to Spain in addition to her own. Up until that moment Columbus had no thought of making any sort of settlement on the island, but with this accident he resolved to leave a large part of the *Santa Maria's* complement to found the first Spanish colony in the New World. The flagship was broken up and her timbers were used in the construction of a fort, erected about five miles east of Cap Haitien and appropriately christened Navidad, because of the date of its inception. Having left thirty-nine devoted sailors to constitute the ancestor of all Latin American colonies, Columbus departed in the *Niña* for Spain on January 4, 1493. Two days later, off Monte Christi, the vagrant *Pinta* was sighted, and the admiral was glad enough to have a consort for the voyage home to swallow at least some of his thoroughly justified anger against the treacherous Pinzon.

Since both ships by now were in bad condition, they sailed into Samana Bay on the extreme northeast of Hispaniola to refit. Here hostile Indians attacked them, and although his vessels needed caulking badly, the admiral felt justified in risking an Atlantic crossing in mid-winter—a risk which nearly brought him to a watery grave. On January 16 the ships left the unfriendly anchorage and steered for home. For more than three weeks they had good weather and splendid sailing, with daily runs even exceeding those of the outward passage, but in February a gale of terrifying intensity battered them for days. The *Pinta* as usual went her own way, and the *Niña* struggled into the shelter of Santa Maria in the Azores. After a respite of ten days the crippled ship was on her way again, only to run into weather even more foul than before. March 3 was the worst day of the entire voyage, but the following morning the gallant little *Niña* struggled over the bar at Lisbon. She was boarded shortly thereafter by Bartholomew Dias, acting in the name of King John.[5] A week or so before, the *Pinta* had reached Bayona near Vigo; she had not put in at the Azores and had missed the second storm, and so had won the race. Her selfish commander sought to steal Columbus' glory by beseeching an audience with his sovereigns, but he rightfully received a complete snub. He sailed the *Pinta* down to his native Palos and died almost immediately, probaby to the benefit of all concerned.

So ended Columbus' crowning achievement; his three subsequent voyages seem anti-climatic in comparison, for his five weeks' passage from the Canaries to the Bahamas did indeed prove the turning point in man's slowly progressing knowledge of the globe. News of his wonder-ful—if misunderstood—discoveries was joyfully received in Spain. He

[5] This is the same Dias who rounded the tip of Africa in 1488.

had not found what he sought, but he was convinced that he had found it. But he had discovered regions whose tropical beauty and luxuriant fertility beggared description, and when in April 1493 Columbus, accompanied by a group of quaintly clad, red-skinned Indians, was received in Barcelona by the sovereigns of Aragon and Castile—to be named Admiral of the Ocean Sea and Viceroy of the Indies, with all the prerogatives and privileges set forth in the capitulation—that indeed was the most glorious moment of his career.

Elsewhere in Europe knowledge of Columbus' discovery spread quickly; his own account (the famous *Columbus Letter*) was published not only in Barcelona but in Rome, Paris, and Basel as well, and a petition was sent to Pope Alexander VI for a confirmation to the Spanish crown of the newly discovered islands, in order to obviate possible Portuguese claims. This led to the issuance of the famous Bull instituting a Line of Demarcation running from north to south a hundred leagues west of the Azores, to the west of which the Spaniards were authorized to explore, and to the east of which the Portuguese received the monopoly of discovery. This line was later adjusted to three hundred and seventy leagues west of the Cape Verde Islands, this being chosen as a half-way mark between the Azores and the newly discovered lands; thus it was that the bulge of Brazil was brought within the Portuguese sphere.[6]

Second Voyage

Columbus now had the wholehearted backing of the Spanish throne, and during his audience at Barcelona it was decided to equip and send out a second voyage as soon as possible. Whereas his first venture was undertaken with a handful of men in three ships small even by the modest standards of the time, the admiral now found himself in command of a mighty armada of seventeen ships, carrying fifteen hundred men—sailors, artisans, colonists, officials, and churchmen, who had flocked to his standard in the hope of sharing in the riches of the Indies. Many figures destined to fame enlisted to serve under him; such as Alonso de Ojeda, who became one of Columbus' most daring successors; Juan de la Cosa, chartmaker and explorer; Ponce de Leon, the discoverer of Florida; Diego Columbus, the admiral's younger brother; Dr. Diego Chanca, the surgeon of the expedition and also its historian.

[6] An earlier pope, as we have seen, had rewarded Portuguese exploring initiative by granting them all newly discovered lands. Pope Alexander VI, a Spanish Borgia, now gave Spain the new discoveries to the westward, with the Line of Demarcation pushed further west, at Tordesillas in 1494.

After Columbus' experience with insubordination on the First Voyage, the Pinzon family were passed over, but various of the faithful Niños appear as masters and pilots. In truth, it was the Grand Fleet.

On September 25, 1493, the imposing squadron sailed from Cadiz, calling at the Canaries for fresh supplies, and leaving Ferro for the main crossing on October 13. Fortune favored Columbus even more than it had the previous year; amid glorious weather a steady wind blew the fleet across the ocean in the remarkable time of three weeks. On November 3 the landfall was made at Dominica, after which the admiral steered northwestward, keeping just inside the beautiful Leeward Islands. A stop of six days was made at Guadeloupe, where a shore party was lost in the tropical jungles. The search for it, though ultimately successful, delayed the voyage. In consequence Columbus pushed on quickly, discovering the many lovely isles of the group and giving them names which in most cases have survived to this day. Anchorages were made at Nevis and Saint Croix, and the fleet put in for several days at the southwestern tip of Puerto Rico. They finally sighted Hispaniola and coasted its northern shore, but when they reached Navidad on November 27, they found that the entire colony had been wiped out by the Indians. The admiral then proposed a new site for the colony, and a place to the east of Monte Cristi was selected, as being near the reputed gold mines of an interior district called the Cibao. Here, about seventy miles from Navidad along the coast, the settlement of Isabela was founded in the opening days of 1494, named appropriately for the puissant sovereign whose patronage had made the discovery of a New World possible.

Having established this infant township and made a reconnaissance inland to the Cibao, Columbus set forth on what, without too much facetiouness, might be called the first West Indies cruise. With him were picked men and three small vessels suitable for inshore navigation, including his old favorite *Niña*. In late April the ships left Isabela, and after coasting the now-familiar shores of Hispaniola, steered for Cape Maisi, the eastern tip of Cuba. Columbus was still keenly on the trail of the Grand Khan and Prester John. His course lay close inshore along the ironbound south coast of Cuba, past Guantanamo and the site of Santiago to Cabo de Cruz at the western end. As he cruised along, he learned from natives of the existence of a rich and beautiful island to the south, so he stood away from Cuba and sighted the gorgeous coast line of Jamaica on May 5. His first port of call was St. Ann's Bay, which he was to know only too well in the period of his deepest distress years later. From there he proceeded westward as far as Montego Bay, thinking the land "the fairest island that eyes have beheld."

On May 13 he returned to Cabo de Cruz and then sailed to explore the whole southern coast of Cuba. As Columbus made his way among the archipelago of small islands which lies to the south of the Cuban mainland, his mind harked back to Sir John Mandeville, who had written that there were five thousand islands in the Indies, and the ever-elusive Orient seemed near at hand. Columbus, with poetic felicity, named these islands El Jardin de la Reina, or the Queen's Garden. His course led him to the western knob of Cuba near Cape Frances. This was his farthest point, and concluding that the land beyond was the Golden Chersonese, he set sail eastward. He coasted the Isle of Pines, beat to windward to Cabo de Cruz, then held his course a second time for Jamaica. From Montego Bay he proceeded counter-clockwise around the island, anchoring every night and trading with the natives who came alongside in their huge seagoing canoes. Sailing direct from Portland Bight to the Blue Mountains, he missed Kingston Harbor, and having cleared Morant Point, he steered for the south coast of Hispaniola. His course took him right around that island, past Cape San Rafael, past Las Flechas where he had harbored with Pinzon on the First Voyage, to Isabela, which he reached the end of September, after an absence of five months.

Much had happened at the little frontier outpost since his departure; the history of Isabela during those months was one of sickness, death, scarcity, threatened mutiny—and endless trouble with the Indians. His youngest brother, Diego, and an incompetent wastrel named Margarit had been left in charge during his absence; they had been wretchedly unequal to the job and the colony was foundering. Columbus' middle brother, Bartholomew, had come out from Spain that summer; he was a strong man and an administrator of some ability, though given to cruelty. Still, his presence seemed to promise hope for better things. The following year a royal commission arrived, who assumed arrogant authority, and six months later Columbus—a weary and discouraged man —returned to Spain in the faithful Niña, leaving Bartholomew in charge. Bartholomew very wisely abandoned the ill-fated and unhappy settlement of Isabela, and transferred the colonists to a more propitious site on the south coast, which as Santo Domingo (or currently Ciudad Trujillo) remains today as the oldest town of European origin in the Western Hemisphere.[7]

Before taking leave of the explorations during the period of Columbus' second visit to America, we might notice one narrative which is at least more circumstantial than hypothetical. There is plausible evidence

[7] Since the assassination of the Dominican dictator Trujillo, in 1961, the name has been restored to the traditional Santo Domingo.

from the celebrated Sneyd-Thacher Manuscript in the Library of Congress that five ships sailed southward from Hispaniola in the autumn of 1494 and fell in with the South American coast near Margarita, to follow it as far as Panama or beyond. The existence of this voyage has by no means met with universal acceptance, but if it did take place, that would mean that the American mainland was discovered four years earlier than the date usually assigned: August 1, 1498, on Columbus' Third Voyage.

Third Voyage

Columbus' reception at court was all that could be expected; he brought with him an Indian king decorated with a heavy gold chain, and he announced that he had found Solomon's Ophir—and he received a generous welcome from his sovereigns, along with a fresh confirmation of privileges. But no eager crowd of volunteers flocked to his standard, for the enthusiasm of 1493 had vanished. For two years the wearied visionary struggled to get a new fleet together, and at last in the spring of 1498 (almost to a week of da Gama's arrival in Calicut) he sailed from San Lucar at the mouth of the Guadalquivir with only six ships. On the Third Voyage the fleet called first at Madeira before proceeding to the usual jumping-off point, the Canaries. From Gomera three vessels were dispatched direct to Hispaniola, and the admiral with the three that were left continued down the West African coast to the Cape Verde Islands. Columbus did this because he had been impressed by the opinion of the Portuguese king that a large land mass lay athwart the Equator, somewhere in the Western Ocean, and he therefore wanted to discover lands lying south of the Antilles. In charting a course for this venture, Columbus anticipated the rule-of-thumb navigation of West Indian skippers of a later date: "South till the butter melts, and then due west."

His outward crossing, however, was the poorest so far. He encountered many calms and blistering hot weather, and it was not until the last day of July that his lookouts sighted the triple peaks of Trinidad. Columbus' intuition was justified, for he had found the southern land mass, as the low shores of Venezuela hove in view off the port bow. His course took him through the Serpent's Mouth into the Gulf of Paria; he spent some days in exploring the Paria Peninsula, which he claimed for Spain, and then leaving by the Dragon's Mouth, he sailed past Margarita to Hispaniola. From the great volume of water flowing from the mouths of the Orinoco, he rightly concluded that the land must be of continental dimensions, since no island could have such a watershed.

But even here his perverse medievalism destroyed his rationalization, for he was convinced that the Orinoco flowed from the Terrestrial Paradise. This curious presumption he reached by holding that the earth was in fact not a true sphere, but was slightly pear-shaped; that a projection like the stem of a pear rose toward Heaven at the Equator, and that the Earthly Paradise lay at the top of this projection. From this premise he argued that he had reached the End of the East. Be that as it may, Columbus' discovery of Venezuela and Trinidad was a substantial one, but it was to be the only geographical contribution of the third voyage.

Affairs in Hispaniola were in a parlous state when he arrived, for even his brother Bartholomew had failed to govern the mutinous and starving colonists, who when not fighting the Indians had been fighting each other. Such bad accounts indeed had filtered across the ocean that the king and queen had sent out a commissioner named Bobadilla, who in October 1500 packed off all three Columbus brothers to Spain—in chains. Although Columbus had failed as a colonial administrator and had consequently lost popularity throughout Spain, he never wholly forfeited the confidence of his sovereigns—Queen Isabella in particular—who realized his uncanny skill as a navigator and his ability as a discoverer. The queen therefore released him from his chains and consented to send him out on another venture, to be devoted to exploration, and thus one for which the admiral was perfectly suited. This final voyage is notable in the annals of discovery; as Columbus had been the first to reach the Antilles in 1492 and the Spanish Main in 1498, so was he now the first to explore the coastal region of Central America—and he was also the first to come into contact with the remarkable Indian civilization of the Mexican periphery.

Fourth Voyage

In the spring of 1502 Columbus sailed from Seville with four fair-sized caravels, and after putting in at Arzilla on the Moroccan coast to relieve a Portuguese garrison besieged by the Moors, he continued his course to the Canaries. His ocean crossing was the best he ever made: twenty-one days from Grand Canary to Martinique, which was sighted (and discovered) on June 15. A run down the chain of the Leeward Islands brought his ships to Santo Domingo by the end of the mouth, where, however, he was forbidden to land by the governor. There was a large fleet in the harbor of Santo Domingo, ready to sail for Spain. Columbus, with his uncanny flair as a navigator, had an almost psychic hunch that a hurricane was in the making and sought to persuade the leaders to put off their departure. But these men, who had no love for the admiral, refused to listen to his advice, and shortly after their departure Columbus had the cold satisfaction of learning that most of the fleet, including his old enemy Bobadilla, had gone to the bottom. Columbus rode out the storm off Santo Domingo; it was a terror but his ships survived, and under the circumstances he was allowed by the governor to repair his damaged vessels. It would seem that at this time he met some of the crews of Rodrigo de Bastidas' expedition, just returned from a cruise along the Spanish Main as far as the Isthmus of Panama, and their information must have enlightened him considerably about the lands to the south.

He left Santo Domingo in mid-July, passed Jamaica to the south, and steered by the Cayman Islands to Honduras. At the island of Bonacca off the Honduras coast he encountered a great canoe laden with merchandise; its well-built cabin was filled with people dressed in dyed cotton, who had weapons and domestic utensils of copper. They said they had brought these things from the West, that is, Yucatan. Here was Columbus within sight of the culture of the Mayas and the Aztecs, but instead of being drawn westward by these evidences of wealth and ingenuity, he persevered in his original intention of following the land in the other direction. Ironically, therefore, this was to be his only glimpse of the wonders which awaited his successors.

Perhaps he later regretted his decision; at all events his passage along the northern shoulder of Honduras must have been a soul-destroying piece of navigation—beating to windward in the teeth of a never-ending rainy gale and making good a run of less than two hundred miles in a month. Only the admiral's iron determination to seek a strait to nearby India and China kept the fleet going throughout this ordeal. Once around the cape, thankfully named Gracias a Dios by the admiral, the expedition had better going, and after coasting along Nicaragua, Columbus put in for a few days at the present site of Puerto Limon, Costa Rica, to give his exhausted crews a well-earned rest. The fleet next explored the Chiriqui Lagoon, ever hopeful that it would be a short-cut to the tantalizingly elusive Orient. They then coasted Veragua, where some gold was found and evidences of more gold, and pushed on amid wet and tempestuous weather past the future site of Nombre de Dios. Still, the land seemed unrewarding and the Indians hostile, so the admiral decided to return to the gold mines of Veragua. They spent Christmas at what is now the entrance of the Panama Canal, and early in January 1503 Columbus selected a site for a settlement at Belem, about fifty miles to the west. Rather more than three months sufficed to mark the rise and fall of this colony; the natives were furiously hostile;

they ambushed and massacred to a man a party sent to fill the water-casks, and on another occasion Bartholomew Columbus, the governor of the new settlement, was severely wounded. After much danger and suffering, as well as anxious delay owing to stormy weather on the surf-beaten coast, the survivors were taken on board and the enterprise was abandoned.

The expedition was by no means out of danger, as the ships had been cruising for a year under the hardest possible usage, so that the crews were literally "at sea in a sieve." Two of the four ships were abandoned on the Central American coast and the remaining two were actually falling apart; yet there was nothing for Columbus to do but struggle back to Hispaniola. At length, having got as far as the northern coast of Jamaica, it became evident that the ships could not stay afloat more than a few hours longer. The admiral ran the two vessels ashore at St. Ann's Bay, which had been his first anchorage in the island nine years previously. Here Columbus was fated to be marooned for an entire year and to face a full-scale mutiny, while one of his devoted followers, Diego Mendez, paddled a canoe all the way to Hispaniola for help. At last, in June 1504, help arrived, and Columbus and his surviving seamen were delivered from their island prison. Well might the gallant Mendez, in his dying days, direct that a canoe be carved on his tombstone!

Broken in body and spirit, Columbus reached Spain for the last time shortly before the death of his great patron, Queen Isabella (November 24, 1504). Although he was only in his mid-fifties, his exertions, mental and physical, had aged and exhausted him before his time. In May 1506, while the court was at Valladolid, he died there—the greatest of all discoverers, but probably convinced to the last that the lands he had discovered were Asiatic. Although in his later years he had been treated with injustice and unfairly deprived of his rights, he was by no means indigent, as he received a fair share of the royal dues from the West Indian revenues. His sons, Diego and Fernando, were educated as pages at court, and Diego was destined to become not only admiral and viceroy but also to marry a relative of the king.

In little more than a decade, the four Columbian and five post-Columbian voyages had revealed the coast line continuously from Honduras to Pernambuco and even beyond, and every island in the West Indies of any importance, except Barbados, had been discovered. Not all the captains and navigators who sailed these seas in the early days could have possessed the warped Medievalism of Columbus; and many, more critical than he, must have realized that these lands were

not Asiatic but were part of a New World. However, it remained for
Amerigo Vespucci to go on record as saying so.[8] After Ojeda's expedition
Vespucci passed into Portuguese service, and in 1501 he was sent on a
voyage to extend Cabral's discoveries of the preceding year.[9] This mission took him down the Brazilian coast from Cape São Roque; it is said
that he reached the mouth of the River Plate, and may have continued
down even as far as Patagonia. It was this voyage, as well as his earlier
venture with Ojeda, that caused the geographer and humanist Martin
Waldseemüller to regard him as the true discoverer of the Western
Hemisphere, and so prompted that scholar to bestow on our continents
the name AMERICA.

NOTES

German Arcinegas, *Amerigo and the New World: The Life and Times of
Amerigo Vespucci*, New York, 1955.

Samuel E. Morison, *Admiral of the Ocean Sea: A Life of Christopher
Columbus*, Boston, 1942; *Christopher Columbus, Mariner*, Boston,
1955; *Portuguese Voyages to America*, Boston, 1940.

MAGELLAN—
THE FIRST CIRCUMNAVIGATION *

C. E. Nowell

*Care has to be taken in describing the third of the "big three" voyages
of exploration. Its leader, Ferdinand Magellan, did not go all the way. He
was killed in the Philippines; but one of his ships, the* Victoria, *continued on through the East Indies and around the Cape of Good Hope
to complete in 1522 the first circumnavigation of the world. The voyage*

* C. E. Nowell, *The Great Discoveries and the First Colonial Empires* (Ithaca,
N.Y.: Cornell University Press, 1954) pp. 57–62. Copyright 1954, by Cornell
University, used by permission of Cornell University Press.

[8] Amerigo Vespucci was a socially prominent Italian from Florence, originally
sent out by the Medici family to watch out for their investments.

[9] Vasco da Gama, in the first voyage around Africa to India, set the pattern
of sailing well across the South Atlantic to take advantage of the prevailing winds.
Cabral, on the second Portuguese voyage to India, actually reached the tip of
Brazil.

revealed to Europe the size of the Pacific Ocean and definitely demon-
strated that the world was not flat.

The original impulse for the voyage came from the discovery by the
Spaniard Balboa of what he called a "South Sea" beyond America.
Magellan, a Portuguese, had served in Portugal's new empire in the
East, but fell out of favor with his king. It was Charles V, King of Spain
and ruler of much else, who sent him on this exploratory voyage. Magel-
lan's name is still prominently preserved in the strait that separates South
America from the island Tierra del Fuego, with Cape Horn at its tip.

The Portuguese Magellan (1480–1521) was the next to take up the
search. After serving under Albuquerque and other renowned commanders in the East for several years, he became disgruntled with
Portuguese policies and with his own failure to achieve promotion.[1]
A letter from his friend Francisco Serrão, then living on Ternate in the
Moluccas, convinced him that those valuable spice islands, which Portugal still had not seized, lay in the zone assigned to Castile at Tordesillas
and led him to offer his services to Spain. Not only did he have the
tempting possession of the Moluccas to offer the Spaniards, but he had
what he considered an even greater prize. Portuguese seamen, sailing
near the Ryukyu Islands north of Formosa, had brought back exag-
gerated reports of their riches and civilization. Magellan heard and
believed these reports, and somehow identified the Ryukyus with the
Old Testament Tarshish and Ophir, from which the ships of Solomon
and Hiram of Tyre had brought back their celebrated wealth.

His main problem was to reach these eastern islands by water without crossing the Eastern Hemisphere, which the treaty had assigned to
Portugal. He soon adopted the theory of a southern strait, though it
is impossible to say how much of the plan he took from Vespucci and
Solís and how much he evolved himself. He accepted the now fairly
general belief that the Pacific, recently seen from Darien by Balboa,
was the eastern arm of the Indian Ocean, since, like others of his time,
he did not restrict the Indian Ocean to its actual limits but thought
of it as extending eastward past the Moluccas. He believed that the
Moluccas lay not far west of the Spanish colonies on the isthmus.
Magellan thus failed to take account of the width of the still unexplored
Pacific.

In 1517 he arrived in Spain to try his fortunes there. His past career
and personal appearance might well have argued against him. There
were several flaws in his Portuguese service record; Albuquerque had

---

[1] Alfonso de Albuquerque did more than anyone else to build the Portuguese
empire in the East.

written a bad report concerning him, and King Manuel considered him a questionable character unworthy of further employment. He looked unprepossessing, being short, squat, and rather ugly; he limped from an old leg wound and had scarcely a coin in his pockets. Despite all handicaps, he was soon to eclipse the fame of Albuquerque and to cost his erstwhile sovereign many sleepless nights.

Magellan first explained his plan to responsible Spanish officials, who hesitated. But the young ruler Charles V, grandson of Ferdinand and Isabella, was attracted by the ambitious idea. He gave an affirmative order and wheels were set in motion to prepare the expedition. Magellan received five ships with suitable equipment and crews. He considered Portuguese seamen generally superior to Spanish, and although there existed some basis for his belief, he enlisted so many that the authorities were obliged to call a halt. With a company finally consisting mostly of Spaniards, he left the port of Sanlúcar in 1519 and headed for South America.

Magellan coasted Brazil, explored the Río de la Plata less fatefully and no more successfully than Solis [2] and passed the first winter in a Patagonian roadstead. Here mutiny flared, not from the sailors but from Spanish officers whose loyalty had been tampered with by certain opponents of Magellan's plan in Spain. The commander, taken by surprise at first, quickly learned which men he could rely on and skillfully used them to regain the upper hand and to restore discipline. He dealt punishment to the ringleaders but pardoned their followers and won most of them over.[3] When the weather turned warmer, he resumed the voyage and soon reached the waterway ever since known as the Strait of Magellan. After a brief hesitation, the voyagers entered the strait and explored its many branches. The southern shore they named Tierra del Fuego, for the many fires seen in the distance by night. These were the campfires of the Fuegan Indians, whom the explorers never saw; they kept out of sight in the daytime.

On emerging into the Pacific, which he named because of its apparent serenity, Magellan had three ships left. One had been wrecked off Patagonia; another, in the hands of still recalcitrant mutineers, had deserted in the strait and returned to Spain. The remaining vessels being in fairly good condition, Magellan was free to seek the Moluccas as well as Tarshish and Ophir. He sailed northward for an unknown distance, probably past the equator, before turning west. An Italian passenger,

[2] Juan Diaz de Solis in 1516 discovered the estuary of the Rio de la Plata, and was later eaten by cannibals.

[3] Sixty years later, the English "Sea Dog" Francis Drake, setting out on the second circumnavigation, also executed a prominent troublemaker at almost the same spot.

who kept a journal of the expedition, says the voyagers sighted only two tiny islands in the Pacific before reaching the Marianas. Both proved to be uninhabited and totally barren. The real hardships of the voyage now began. Food ran low, drinking water spoiled, and scurvy prostrated most of the men, there being scarcely enough well hands to work the ships. The death rate was appalling; day after day corpses were committed to the Pacific with whatever slight ceremony the tottering survivors could manage. Rat meat became a luxury and the very maggots that spoiled the dwindling sea biscuit were an article of diet. Brackish and evil-smelling drinking water was avidly consumed, the wine supply having long been exhausted. As month followed month, all thought of mutiny was forgotten; no one had the strength or spirit for it, and the most ignorant sailor could understand that to turn back was hopeless; the only hope of salvation lay in pressing on. The slightest touch of bad weather would have destroyed the fleet during those bitter months, but on that first occasion the Pacific Ocean lived up to its name and remained calm.

Even so, Magellan's expedition was near its last gasp when the inhabited Mariana Islands were sighted. Dark-skinned Micronesian natives darted from shore in their canoes and swarmed aboard the ships, stealing everything they could lay hands on. These light-fingered propensities caused Magellan to name their islands the Ladrones (Thieves). A clash could not be avoided, and the enfeebled Spaniards mustered strength enough to push the islanders off the ships and to follow them ashore and plunder everything edible from a native village. Then, having taught the savages that two could play at the game of thievery, Magellan continued his westward voyage, leaving the Marianas to enjoy for a while longer the isolation that had lasted since the beginning of their inhabitation.

Strengthened by the island food, the Spaniards were able in a few weeks to reach the Philippines, Magellan had a Malayan interpreter aboard, and as he addressed the Filipinos, it could be perceived that some of them understood his words.[4] This meant that the fleet had entered the region generally familiar to the Portuguese; in short, contact had been made with the eastern rim of civilization.

Magellan, hitherto distinguished for his excellent judgment, now committed an act of rashness that cost him his life. After converting a Filipino chieftain to Christianity, he with a few of the Spaniards joined this ally in a war against a neighboring chief. Magellan perished in the combat, and his convert quickly apostatized, killing as many of

---

[4] That interpreter, who had gone from the East Indies to Europe, thus became the first man to sail around the world.

his new white acquaintances as possible and compelling the rest to depart hastily in the ships.

Electing new leaders, the seamen now went on a rather aimless odyssey about the East Indies, until they finally dropped down to the Moluccas. Since the Portuguese had not yet occupied these islands, the Spaniards could fill their holds with a cargo of spice, even though Magellan's old friend Serrão, their expected intermediary, had recently died. Of the three remaining ships, one was now unseaworthy and had to be burned. Another leaked so badly that it was patched up and sent eastward to try the run across the Pacific to the Spanish isthmus of Darien.[5] The third, the Victoria, now commanded by the Biscayan Sebastián de El Cano, was assigned the task of eluding the Portuguese and returning to Spain via the Cape of Good Hope.

The ship bound for Darien, baffled by weather, failed to reach the American coast and turned back to the East Indies, to be captured there by the Portuguese. But El Cano's Victoria, in spite of more starvation experiences, completed the circumnavigation of the globe and returned to Sanlúcar in 1522. The eighteen survivors aboard, who included the Italian chronicler, were at first surprised to learn that they had apparently lost a day in their time reckoning. The discrepancy was explained, however, when "a certayne excellente man . . . who was also a greate Philosopher and Astronomer, answered that it could not otherwyse chaunce unto them, hauynge sayled three years continually, ever folowynge the soone towarde the West."

Importance of Magellan's Voyage

The earth had been circled and the width of the Pacific revealed, even though circumnavigation had not been a part of Magellan's original plan. Since Pythagoras, men had known the earth to be round; now the Victoria, a smaller ship than any in Columbus' squadron, had provided a concrete demonstration. Men could now have some notion, however dim, of the true ratio of land to water on the face of the globe.

The great voyage did not solve all problems or altogether obliterate traces of past erroneous thinking. Scholars would not entirely abandon Ptolemy and continued for years to think of the Pacific as an eastern extension of the Indian Ocean. Their maps showed Asia bending northeastward from Malaya and joining America not far north of where Magellan had crossed the Pacific. In this notion, of course, there was a crude approximation to the truth, and the voyages of Vitus Bering in

[5] Panama.

the eighteenth century showed that Asia and North America did in fact miss connection by only a few miles.

NOTES

Charles E. Nowell (ed.), *Magellan's Voyage Around the World: Three Contemporary Accounts*, Ithaca, 1962.

Charles M. Parr, *So Noble a Captain: The Life and Times of Ferdinand Magellan*, New York, 1953 (*Ferdinand Magellan, Circumnavigator* in 1964 edition).

Katherine Romoli, *Balboa of Darien, Discover of the Pacific*, Garden City, 1953.

William L. Schurz, *The Manila Galleon*, New York, 1939 (paper, 1959).

THE FRENCH IN INLAND AMERICA *

Edward Heawood

The earliest important exploration of the interior of North America was undertaken in the Southwest by Coronado and other Spaniards in a frustrating quest for gold. The most important work, however, was carried on by the French in the seventeenth century. At the outset, Samuel Champlain established Port Royal in the present Nova Scotia in 1605 and then Quebec, in its commanding position on the St. Lawrence, in 1608. He penetrated to some distance into the interior, discovering the lake that bears his name and running afoul of the Iroquois. He explored as far as Lake Ontario and died in 1635.

The great spread of French influence into the interior, as described in the following pages, was the work of a few bold explorers, particularly Joliet and Father Marquette in the Great Lakes region and La Salle in the Mississippi; the lower Mississippi had been reached by the Spaniard De Soto more than a century earlier.

The third stage of major inland exploration came around 1800, with the work of the Scot Alexander Mackenzie and the American army officers Lewis and Clark who penetrated all the way to the Pacific.

* Edward Heawood, *A History of Geographical Discovery in the Seventeenth and Eighteenth Centuries* (Cambridge, England: Cambridge University Press, 1912), pp. 107–117. By permission of the Cambridge University Press.

Although the English settlers were behind the French in exploring activity in the more southern regions, in the far north, bordering on the Arctic wilds, Englishmen played a preponderating part in pushing back the bounds of the unknown. The voyages of the Elizabethan navigators at the end of the previous century had brought to light the wide gulf between Greenland and the Continent, with many of its inlets—the entrance to the vast interior basin of Hudson's Bay having been seen by Davis in 1587. In the new century the work was continued first by Waymouth, who appears to have passed within the entrance in 1602, and afterwards by Henry Hudson, who sailed in 1610 (the year following his voyage to the Hudson River) on his last and fatal voyage to the bay which has since borne his name. The voyages of Button (1612–13), Bylot and Baffin (1615), and of the Dane, Jens Munk (1619–20), did much to improve the knowledge of the shores of the bay and of the strait leading to it, though they did not finally disprove the existence of the supposed passage to the Pacific Ocean. Foxe and James however, in 1631–32, showed the extreme improbability that any such passage could be found, though they did not absolutely dispose of the question.

This advance of the English to a point so near, comparatively speaking, to the French settlements in Canada, was bound to lead to rivalry between the two nations. Some knowledge of the interior basin reached the French at an early date, and in 1656 an expedition was despatched from Quebec under Jean Bourdon to take possession of the country bordering on the bay in the name of France. Only 13 years later, after a successful trading voyage had been carried out in 1668 under the auspices of Prince Rupert, the Hudson Bay Company was incorporated by Charter of King Charles II, and a prolonged conflict of jurisdiction between the two nations was the natural result.

We must now return to the history of exploration in Canada after the death of Champlain. Although for some years after that event no very important discoveries were made, the bounds of knowledge were steadily extended, thanks to the restless energy of two very different classes of men—the Jesuit missionaries and the fur traders. The latter, in their constant search for new collecting grounds for the much-prized beaver skins, led the way into distant and hitherto untrodden countries, while the Jesuits were hardly, if at all, behind them in opening up new stations among the outlying tribes of Indians. More is known of the labours of the Jesuits than of the traders, as their journeys were for the most part recorded in the *Relations* published under the auspices of their Order in Paris. In 1641 two of their number, Raymbault and

Jogues, following in the footsteps of Nicollet, reached the Sault Ste Marie, soon to become the base for further discovery towards the west. Here they encountered a large body of Indians, and from them learnt of the existence of the Mississippi (though not by name) and of the Sioux dwelling on its banks. In 1642 Jogues was captured by a band of Iroquois and taken south by Lake Champlain and its continuation Lake George, of which, after his release, he was able to give a more correct idea than had before prevailed. The fear inspired by the invincible Iroquois confederacy still stood in the way of a better knowledge of the two lowest of the Great Lakes, and only after a peace had been patched up with them in 1653 was the south shore of Ontario explored by Father Poncet, who had undertaken the work of evangelisation among that warlike race.

In the following year Father Le Moyne penetrated farther into their country by way of the Oswego River, hearing vague but stimulating reports of the countries to the south-west. An advance was also made about this time in the work of western discovery. In 1654 two traders are said to have visited the country beyond Lake Michigan, and in 1658 the field was taken by an enterprising pioneer named Groseilliers, who reached Lake Superior, and, returning the following year with his brother-in-law Radisson, explored the southern shores of that lake. In their further wanderings they may even have reached the Mississippi itself. In 1660 Groseilliers was accompanied by a Jesuit named Ménard, who, after a winter on Lake Superior, started southward to seek the scattered Hurons who had fled to this remote district after the destruction of their nation by the Iroquois in 1649. Ménard never returned and his fate is involved in uncertainty. In 1665 an important step was taken in the founding of a mission station at La Pointe near the west extremity of Lake Superior. This was accomplished by Father Allouez, who for the first time heard of the great western river as the "Missipi," obtaining also vague accounts of the western plains from bands of Sioux with whom he came in contact. A few years later Allouez transferred his labours to the neighbourhood of Green Bay on Lake Michigan, and in 1670 penetrated to the Wisconsin, which, he heard, led to the Mississippi, a great river more than a league wide. His place had been taken on Lake Superior by Father Marquette, whose name occupies an important place in subsequent discovery, and who also collected information as to the mysterious countries to the south-west, through which he believed the great river to flow to the Pacific.

Meanwhile important changes had taken place in the government of New France, which in 1663 had reverted to the French crown. Supported by the great minister Colbert, the new officials, especially the

Intendant, Talon, displayed much energy in extending French influence into the outlying districts. In 1669 Talon sent Joliet—soon to take a prominent place in the history of exploration—to search for the copper mines of Lake Superior. Although unsuccessful in his search, Joliet did good work by opening up, on his return journey, a new route to the west, *via* Lake Erie and the channel connecting it with Lake Huron. Again, in 1671, Talon despatched a great expedition under St Lusson to the Sault Ste Marie to take formal possession of the country thereabouts in presence of the assembled Indians. With St Lusson were associated both Joliet and Nicholas Perrot, the latter one of the most enterprising of the French adventurers at the time.

About the same time explorers were also busy in the districts bordering on the colony to the north. In 1660 Fathers Dablon and Druillettes had reached the sources of the Saguenay, while much further west Groseilliers and Radisson had reached Lake Nipigon, and one of their followers named Péré had crossed the divide separating Lake Superior from Hudson Bay.

Subsequent differences with the authorities induced Groseilliers to enter into association with the English, and in 1664 and 1668 he made voyages with Captain Gillam to Hudson Bay, the promising results of which led to the foundation of the Hudson Bay Company. In 1671 Talon entrusted Father Albanel with a mission to the north by way of the Saguenay, and in 1672 the Jesuit reached the shores of the northern basin, which were taken over in the name of the French king.

But already a new actor had appeared on the scene, who though relying mainly on his own resources was to surpass the achievements of all his contemporaries. This was Robert Cavelier de la Salle, who in 1666 reached Canada, bent on seeking his fortune. His elder brother was already in the country, and the seminary of St Sulpice, to which he belonged, was at the time in possession of seignioral rights over Montreal and the lands in its neighbourhood. The future explorer obtained from the seminary the grant of a large tract of land at La Chine, a few miles from Montreal. While resident here his enthusiasm was excited by stories brought by Indians of the unexplored lands to the south-west, and he resolved to undertake an exploring journey in that direction. Having sold his concession at La Chine, La Salle started in 1669 in company with the Sulpicians, Dollier and Galivée, and, navigating Lake Ontario, reached the Niagara River, where they heard for the first time the roar of the great cataract. Meeting with Joliet on his way from the Upper Lakes, the priests were induced to take a route in that direction, while La Salle, whose thoughts were turned towards the south, determined to carry out his explorations separately. The priests reached the Sault Ste Marie by Joliet's route, but returned by the Ottawa, the principal result of the journey being the improved knowledge of Lake Erie, and its position in the great Laurentian system, supplied by Galivée's journal and map. La Salle's proceedings after he left the priests are involved in much obscurity, and have been the subject of conflicting views on the part of historians. On the authority of a somewhat questionable document it has been claimed that either in 1669–70 or in 1671 he actually reached the Mississippi, but this is almost certainly incorrect. It seems probable that the traveller discovered the Ohio in 1669 and descended it for some distance, perhaps to the rapids at Louisville. It may also be the case that in 1671 he explored the southern part of Lake Michigan and reached the Illinois. That he reached the Mississippi on this occasion is negatived by the absence of all claim to this discovery on his behalf until some years after the authenticated journey of Marquette and Joliet, with which we have now to deal.

The energetic Talon was recalled soon after the arrival of the Comte de Frontenac as Governor in 1672. Before his departure he had entrusted to Joliet the work of discovering the great western river of which so much had been heard, and tracing it to its mouth either in the Gulf of Mexico or the Pacific Ocean. The new governor lent his support to the proposed expedition, which started in the summer of 1672, proceeding first to the Strait of Mackinaw (then known as Michillimackinac) at the entrance to Lake Michigan. Here he was joined by the Jesuit Marquette, who had for two years been in charge of a mission station on the north side of the strait. On reaching the head of Green Bay the two explorers ascended the Fox past Lake Winnebago and, obtaining guides from the Mi'amis, crossed the divide and reached the waters of the Wisconsin. Floating down this stream they reached the Mississippi in a week, and the great stream which had been the subject of so many speculations was at last seen by Europeans. Passing on through an uninhabited tract, they reached the great prairies roamed over by herds of "buffalo." Still floating down the great river they entered into friendly relations with the Illinois, passed the river of the same name, and soon afterwards the rocky cliffs then decorated with painted monsters representing the Indian gods. The farthest point reached was near the mouth of the Arkansas, where they narrowly escaped an attack from the tribe of that name. Hence they retraced their course, having done enough to prove that the great river must enter the Gulf of Mexico, though many miles of its winding channel still lay between them and its mouth. Ascending the Illinois the voyagers crossed over to the south end of Lake Michigan and reached Green Bay at the end of September, 1673.

Although much weakened by dysentery, Marquette returned in 1674 to the Illinois to establish a mission on its banks, but succumbed to his malady on the shores of Lake Michigan when retracing his steps in 1675. Joliet subsequently did good work in other directions, journeying to Hudson Bay in 1679, and while engaged in the fisheries acquiring a close knowledge of the St. Lawrence and the coasts of Labrador, which gained him the post of Royal pilot and hydrographer.

To Joliet and Marquette belongs the merit of the first discovery of the Mississippi [1] but the opening up of its valley to French enterprise was due to the ambitious and far-sighted views of La Salle, who saw in these vast and fertile regions a field far surpassing in promise the frost-bound shores of the St. Lawrence.

Thwarted throughout by the jealousy and dislike of his fellow colonists, La Salle found a supporter in the Governor Frontenac, himself far from popular in the colony. A fort having been established by the governor on Lake Ontario, La Salle obtained a grant of the fort and the surrounding lands, and thus secured to himself the important trade which it commanded. Here he matured his schemes, which aimed at nothing less than the colonisation of the fertile plains of the Mississippi valley, and the conversion of the Indian tribes and their transformation into peaceful subjects of the French crown. Obtaining a patent from the king, by which he was authorised to continue his discoveries towards the south, and to secure the country explored by the construction of forts, La Salle obtained the co-operation of an Italian officer then in France named Henri de Tonty, whose unswerving loyalty proved of priceless value amid the general opposition and treachery which beset the enterprise. Another coadjutor who played a prominent part in it and became the chronicler of the expedition was the Recollet friar Louis Hennepin, a Fleming by birth, who, already stationed at Fort Frontenac, now obtained permission to accompany the expedition. Hennepin, though not lacking in courage, was of a vain and boastful disposition, and grave doubts exist as to the trustworthiness of his account, which is, however, of some value as supplementing the other records.

With the aid of his associates—one of whom, La Motte by name, took part in the early stages only of the expedition—La Salle in the autumn of 1678 transported his supplies to the Niagara River, where a fort was established and a small vessel built above the cataract, of which a minute account is given for the first time in Hennepin's journal. After a winter of great hardship the vessel—named the *Griffin,* in allusion to

[1] Theirs was not actually the first discovery, since the Spaniard Hernando De Soto had reached the lower part of the river in 1541.

the arms of Frontenac—was ready for launching, and the navigation of the upper lakes began.

The party had now been increased by the arrival of two more Recollet friars, Fathers Membré and Ribourde. Harassed by intrigue and desertions, as well as by anxiety in regard to his creditors in the colony, La Salle slowly made his way past the Strait of Mackinaw and along the shores of Lake Michigan, encountering constant storms, and meeting with some difficulties from the Indians. The *Griffin* had meanwhile been sent back with a cargo of furs, while Tonty, who had been sent to the Sault Ste Marie, only arrived after much delay at the fort of the Mi'amis built by La Salle at the mouth of the St Joseph. It was not till December, 1679, that a start could be made up the St Joseph for the portage to the Kankakee, down which river the voyage was pursued to the Illinois, until an encampment of that nation was reached. Still pursued by intrigue and desertion, and threatened with ruin by the loss of the *Griffin* either by storm or treachery, La Salle returned for fresh succour, leaving his small force under Tonty with instructions to commence the building of another vessel at a newly-constructed fort which he named Crèvecœur in token of the low ebb of his fortunes.

After a winter journey of incredible hardships La Salle reached the French settlements and raised funds for the renewal of his undertaking, only to learn of the desertion of the greater part of the men left with Tonty. That officer with two or three faithful followers became involved in an invasion of the Illinois country by the Iroquois, and only after great sufferings made their way back by the west shores of Michigan, just when La Salle was bringing aid to them by the opposite side. After a vain search for his followers, during which the Illinois was descended to the Mississippi, La Salle wintered at Fort Mi'ami, engaged in the re-organisation of his enterprise, which had now to start afresh form the beginning. Meanwhile Hennepin, who with two companions, Accault and Du Gay, had been despatched from Fort Crèvecœur on an exploring trip down the Illinois, had ascended the Upper Mississippi and undergone many adventures among the Sioux, by whom he was captured. The exact extent of his journeys cannot be determined owing to the suspicion which attaches to his veracity. In a second edition of his work, published after La Salle's death, he made the fraudulent claim to the discovery of the whole Mississippi to the sea, but his pretended descriptions are known to have been borrowed from the journal of Father Membré, who accompanied La Salle on his successful journey of 1681. While on the Upper Mississippi Hennepin fell in with an enterprising French pioneer, Du Luth (or Du Lhut) by name, who had for two years been exploring near the head of Lake

Superior and the head-waters of the Mississippi.[2] He had thus preceded Hennepin in his visit to the Sioux towns, and it is apparently from one of his companions that Lake Pepin derives its name. In his company Hennepin made his way to Green Bay and Mackinac, and thence to Montreal, his connection with La Salle now finally ceasing.

Having guarded against danger from the Iroquois by forming a defensive alliance between the Mi'amis and Illinois, La Salle returned to Canada to complete his arrangements for a final attempt to descend the Mississippi to the sea. At Mackinac he met with Tonty and Membré, who again joined him, whereupon, in December 1681, the re-organised expedition once more set out from Fort Mi'ami, and, descending the Illinois in canoes, entered the Mississippi in the following February. Floating on past the mouth of the turbid Missouri, the explorers, this time blessed with better fortune, soon reached the Ohio, and on March 13 heard, through the fog which enveloped the stream, the war drums of the Arkansas tribe near the river which now bears their name. Friendly relations were however established and the voyagers passed on, visiting the great town of the Taensas and meeting with a cordial reception from other riverine tribes. Avoiding a hostile demonstration of the Quinipissas, on April 6 they reached the beginning of the great delta, and, dividing their forces, descended the three main channels into which the river divided, uniting again on the shores of the Gulf of Mexico. Here a ceremony was enacted by which La Salle took possession of the whole Mississippi valley in the name of the French king, in honour of whom the vast region received the name of Louisiana.

A great triumph had been won, but a toilsome voyage up the great river still awaited the explorers. During this some fighting occurred, and the leader was prostrated by illness, but travelling by slow degress was able to reach Mackinac before the end of September. In order to develop the resources of his new domain La Salle proposed to found two colonies, one on the Illinois as a centre of the fur trade of that region, and one at the mouth of the Mississippi to secure an outlet in that direction. The former first engaged his attention, and a fort was built on a rock overhanging the Illinois, which received the name of Fort St Louis; around it a large body of Indians soon assembled, seeking protection against the Iroquois foe.

During La Salle's absence a new governor—La Barre—had arrived in Canada, and the explorer soon found cause to lament the loss of his protector Frontenac. Thwarted on all hands he returned to France, and

[2] The city of Duluth, Minnesota, at the western end of Lake Superior, is named for him.

finding favour at court, obtained the support of the king for a new enterprise on the Gulf of Mexico. By undertaking to break the Spanish monopoly on the waters of the gulf he secured the equipment of an expedition of four ships, two of them manned with a force of soldiers and a body of colonists and artificers. Three Recollet friars, Membré, Douay, and Le Clerc, joined the expedition, as well as La Salle's brother already alluded to and two other Sulpicians. The command of the vessels was given to a naval officer, Beaujeu, an unfortunate decision, as the divided command soon led to friction which boded ill for the success of the enterprise. Misfortunes indeed pursued the adventurers from the outset. Delays occurred in the preparations, and when in July, 1684, the expedition sailed, disputes soon broke out between the commanders. During the stay in the West Indies, La Salle was seized with severe illness, which for a time totally incapacitated him. Arrived at length in the gulf, a search was made in vain for the mouth of the Mississippi, of the longitude of which La Salle was ignorant. By an unfortunate mistake he landed his men among the lagoons on the northwestern shore of the gulf, over 400 miles from the object of his search, while to add to his distress the ship laden with all the stores for the colony was wrecked on attempting to enter a neighbouring bay.

A temporary station was established, but disaster still attended the party. The natives were hostile, the crops soon proved a failure, and the one small vessel which remained to La Salle after the departure of Beaujeu suffered the fate of the store-ship. Returning to the temporary fort after a vain attempt to make his way overland to the Mississippi, the leader formed the desperate resolution of leading his party overland to Canada, leaving a few men only to represent him on the gulf. Crossing the prairies, roamed over by herds of buffalo, which occupy the basins of the Brazos, Trinity, and other Texan streams, the expedition had not yet passed into the Mississippi valley, when a tragedy occurred which finally broke up the ill-starred expedition. Discontent had for some time prevailed in the party, and it reached a climax (March, 1687) in the murder, first of La Salle's nephew Moranget and two subordinates, and finally of La Salle himself. The loyal remnant of the party now consisted only of Joutel, a gardener's son, who had throughout shown himself one of the leader's most efficient and trusty lieutenants, with two priests and three youths, one of whom was nephew to La Salle. These were helpless to avenge the murders, but, after some time had been spent among the Cenis Indians, the ringleaders fell at the hands of their own followers and Joutel was able to make his way with

a small party to the Arkansas, where he met with two of Tonty's
subordinates, left by that officer during a descent of the Mississippi in
search of his missing chief. Tonty had even reached the mouth of the
great river a second time while La Salle was engaged in his weary search
for it on the plains of Texas. Joutel now made his way with his
companions to the fort on the Illinois (1687), and it is to his pen that
we owe the best account of the fatal expedition. The memoirs published
by Tonty are a valuable authority for both of La Salle's expeditions in
which he took part, while the results of the discoveries are well shown on
the great map of Franquelin, hydrographer at Quebec, published in
1684.

Two expeditions, undertaken about the time of La Salle's death,
deserve mention. The one, led by Nicholas Perrot, somewhat extended
the bounds of knowledge in the region of the Upper Mississippi, the
other, under De Troyes and Iberville, was directed against the English
on the shores of Hudson Bay. Iberville was soon to take a prominent
place in the history of the French in America.[3]

La Salle's death forms a fitting conclusion to the first great period
of geographical discovery in the interior of North America. Although
some have tried to disparage his services, while his proud and reserved
nature in some degree unfitted him to be a successful leader of men,
there can be nothing but admiration for the indomitable will which
helped him to persevere in the face of untold difficulties in the task
which he had set himself. Although not crowned with success during
his lifetime, his schemes had far-reaching effects on the future of the
Mississippi basin, where his steps were soon followed by his compatriots,
and where, for a time at least, French influence was secure from the
encroachments of rivals. The period which now ensued—ushered in
by the revolution in England—was marked by political rivalries with
that nation and gave little scope for great pioneering journeys, so that the
vast regions of the far west were not thrown open till a much later date.

Throughout the century now closing, the brilliant geographical
achievements in North America were all the work of Frenchmen. For
the very reason which made them more successful as colonists, the
English settlers were less given to the wandering life which carried the
French fur-traders into the remote wilds of the continent; and though
attempts have been made to prove that English explorers entered the
Mississippi basin at an early date, the accounts of their journeys rest
on too insecure a basis to be definitely accepted as facts.

[3] In 1699, Iberville established the first French colony on the Gulf near the
site of Biloxi, Mississippi. In 1718, his brother, Bienville, established New
Orleans.

NOTES

Bern Anderson, *Surveyor of the Seas: The Life and Voyages of Captain George Vancouver,* Seattle, 1960.

Ray A. Billington, *Westward Expansion: A History of the American Frontier,* 2d ed., New York, 1960.

Edward G. Bourne, *The Voyages of Champlain,* 2 Vols., New York, 1922.

J. Bartlett Brebner, *The Explorers of North America,* Garden City, 1933.

Francis Parkman, *Pioneers of France in the New World; The Jesuits in North America; LaSalle and the West,* various editions, Boston.

Alfred L. Rowse, *The Expansion of Elizabethan England,* London, 1956.

James A. Williamson, *The Voyages of the Cabots and the English Discovery of North America under Henry VII and Henry VIII,* Cambridge, England, 1929.

CAPTAIN COOK AND THE SOUTH SEAS *

J. Holland Rose

After the three great voyages of Columbus, da Gama, and Magellan, around 1500, the most significant maritime exploration was the work of Captain James Cook of the British Navy, between 1768 and 1779.

The burst of interest in the Pacific on the part of Britain and France followed closely upon the end of the Seven Years' War in 1763. In that climax of their "Duel for Empire," the British had virtually wrecked the old French colonial empire in Canada, in India, and elsewhere around the world. The desire to make up that loss and to retrieve some of their lost prestige may have inflenced the French in sending out expeditions under Bougainville, La Pérouse, and others. That was enough to give the British an extra interest in the Pacific. Another motive, in both England and France, came from the rapidly increasing curiosity about things scientific. This aspect was especially prominent in the role of Sir Joseph Banks, a wealthy English ameteur naturalist, who was able to exercise political influence in promoting official exploration. He accompanied Cook on his first voyage, which had as its avowed purpose the astronomical observation at Tahiti of the

* J. Holland Rose, *Man and the Sea: Stages in Maritime and Human Progress* (Cambridge, England: W. Heffer & Sons, Ltd., 1935), pp. 183–218. By permission of W. Heffer & Sons, Ltd.

transit of the planet Venus. Banks's interest was also apparent in the naming of Botany Bay in Australia. Cook was picked for his role because he was an expert hydrographer. He and some of the officers he trained —including Vancouver, who would leave his name on the map of America, and Bligh, of the Bounty mutiny—did valuable work in charting the newly discovered areas.

The Pacific had been the scene of some Spanish discoveries, beginning with Balboa and Magellan. The Dutch, in their great period of maritime activity, had also explored those waters, with Abel Tasman actually discovering Australia and New Zealand in the 1640s. England had been represented in the early quests by some able freebooters, Francis Drake and William Dampier, in particular. But that early voyaging had not been followed up to any extent, and it would remain for Cook and his contemporaries to make the world 'South Sea-conscious."

Cook's first voyage had its most significant results in stimulating interest in Australia which he "re-discovered." In 1788, 20 years after his visit, Britain sent out some 1100 convicts to establish a colony of settlement at Sydney; later New Zealand also became a part of the British Empire. His second voyage, in which he sailed back and forth across the Pacific, demonstrated that a supposed great southern continent did not exist. The third voyage led to international rivalry in the Pacific Northwest area. The discovery of sea otter furs there resulted in a lively scramble of Spaniards, British, Americans, and Russians. That third voyage also brought Hawaii, where Cook was killed, to the attention of those nations, just as his first vayage advertised the charms of Tahiti, recently visited by Wallis and then Bougainville.

The eighteenth century witnessed no really important oceanic discoveries until the time of Bougainville and Cook, for Anson's circumnavigation in 1740–2 was more an act of war against Spain than of exploration.[1] Yet in this dull time at sea, trade was expanding apace, ships were growing both in size and in seaworthiness, e.g. the lowering of the poop and the general introduction of the jib (the fore-topmast staysail) helped to keep the ship's head well before the wind in a following gale. No more, then, do we hear of the device, recorded by Dampier, of seamen standing on the bow and holding out their coats wide to help to keep the ship before the wind. Also in 1714 the foundation by our Government [Britain] of the Board of Longitude, and the

---

[1] During the so-called War of Jenkins' Ear, between Britain and Spain, a British squadron under Commodore George Anson set out for the Pacific, where it encountered terrific inroads of scurvy. His flagship completed a circumnavigation, after capturing a rich "Manila Galleon."

resulting inventions of the sextant and chronometer, enabled "masters" to keep time with something like accuracy, and therefore to calculate longitude far more exactly than was possible in the age of Tasman.[2] Consequently, the time was now ripe for clearing up many problems in the remote and hitherto unexplored parts of the oceans, and the gradual increase in the size and comfort of ships, together with improvements in hygiene and food supply, kept crews efficient even to the end of long voyages. Since the time of Sir James Lancaster, East Indiamen were supplied with lime-juice, and were called "lime-juicers." In general, the Royal Navy neglected this cure for scurvy until about 1790.

After the Peace of Utrecht (1713) maritime commerce advanced rapidly, especially that of the slave trade from Africa to the Americas. France also made great efforts to extend her colonies in Africa and North America so that even by the year 1736 her growth aroused general concern. Already, in 1721–22, the Great South Land had been sought by a Dutch seaman, Roggeveen, to the west of South America, where Dampier's chief, Davis, had reported signs of high land. Roggeveen now discovered the mysterious Easter Island, with its vast raised platforms of colossal stone statues. . . . They still defy explanation. But the islanders (who were defenceless) placed their trust wholly, when attacked by the Dutch crew, in these colossal statues. Afterwards Roggeveen re-discovered some Polynesian islands (probably in the Palliser and Society Groups), touched at New Britain and then completed his circumnavigation of the globe—the last great feat of Dutch seamen.

This and other efforts spurred on a French seaman, Pierre Bouvet, in 1739, to find the Southern Continent. Far to the south-south-west of South Africa, in latitude 55° south, he sighted a lofty headland which he assumed to be its northern point. It was a worthless island, now named after him. In 1771 a French navigator, Kerguelen, renewed the search in the south of the Indian Ocean, for a fertile southern land reported vaguely by de Gonneville of Honfleur early in the sixteenth century. He sighted land which, like Bouvet, he hopefully reported as part of the Continent, which would command the sea route to the East Indies. It was the almost uninhabitable Kerguelen Island.

These last efforts, in which mere surmise played far too large a part, scarcely deserve notice here except as explaining why, after her defeat in the Seven Years' War (1756–63), France sought to retrieve her position overseas by a renewal of the age-long quest for the *Terra*

[2] In 1642 the Dutch navigator Abel Tasman discovered the great island now named for him (originally Van Diemen's Land) and also New Zealand, which he named. In 1644 he sailed along the northern coast of Australia and north to Japan.

Australis incognita, which imaginative geographers still endowed with vast resources. Already, in 1756, a French writer, de Brosses, had pointed out that nothing was known of the Southern Pacific, yet in that vast expanse there might exist, as Ptolemy had pointed out about A.D. 150, a great continent peopled by nations as mighty as those of Europe. Let, then, the French acquire those lands, and they would achieve world supremacy, for "he who is master of the sea is master of the land."

In 1766 there came a sharp retort from a Briton, John Callender, who published a book summoning his countrymen, now masters of the seas, to acquire these vast potential resources. Also, about the same time, Alexander Dalrymple, a Scottish merchant and seafarer, who had traded in the East Indies, compiled a survey of the discoveries in the Pacific Ocean up to 1764, which he printed in 1767 and published in 1769. In it he asserted that the Great South Land *had* been discovered on the east side by Juan Fernandez, on the west by Tasman, and elsewhere by others. It therefore only remained to find the intermediate parts; and the whole would comprise "a greater extent than the whole civilised part of Asia, from Turkey eastward to the extremity of China." Here was the final spur to explorations in the South Pacific.

In truth, during man's age-long spread over the oceans, nothing is more singular than his neglect of that vast area. Though fanciful cartographers had for ages filled it with *Terra Australis,* or sea monsters, yet remained *incognita* down to the time of James Cook. Why this long delay? I suggest these three reasons:—(1) After threading the mazy Straits of Magellan, or doubling tempestuous Cape Horn, ships were generally so battered by the prevalent westerly gales, and crews were so weary and scorbutic, that further struggles westwards were unthinkable and sails were gladly set for a run northwards towards more genial climes. Thus, though Dampier had urged the need of stretching on westwards from Cape Horn towards New Holland in order to discover the Great South Land, yet explorers, one and all, stood away to the North, or at most to the North-West. (2) Not only west winds and scurvy, but also the northerly Humboldt current led them to shape their course for that buccaneers' paradise, the isle of Juan Fernandez. About latitude 14° south the current turns north-west and then west across the Pacific Ocean, while another branch of it bears ships to the coast of Mexico, off which (about 14° north) the trade wind and current favour a quick run to the Marshall, Caroline or Ladrone Islands—a course generally followed down to the time of Anson. (3) The precious metals of Peru and Mexico also tempted seamen northwards either to work them or to plunder the vessels that bore the bullion from Acapulco to the Philippines [or] to Spain.[3] Thus Nature and man's greed limited him, during some 150 years, to certain well-marked Pacific routes, and relegated the south of that vast expanse to the domain of vain conjecture or political jealousy.

This was now to be changed, for both British and French expeditions were despatched to the Pacific. The first was that of the Hon. John Byron [4] in H.M.S. *Dolphin* (1764–66), who had orders ultimately to find a strait through from the north of Drake's New Albion [5] to Hudson's Bay, or else return via the Cape of Good Hope. He sailed nowhere near New Albion, but headed north-north-west and then west from the Straits of Magellan to the Ladrones and sighted nothing except a few valueless islets. In 1766–68 Captain Samuel Wallis, in the *Dolphin* sought for the Southern Continent and discovered Tahiti, which he named and annexed as King George's Island, but he accomplished nothing else of importance. . . . His colleague, Carteret, in the little laggard *Swallow,* sighted Pitcairn's Island and a few others near by, and, sailing on westwards, re-discovered the Santa Cruz group; he also found that Dampier's New Britain consisted of two islands; the smaller he named New Ireland. Assailed by the islanders, he had hard work to reach Dutch settlements and was there churlishly treated. Finally, after numberless dangers he reached Spithead in March, 1769.

Compared with these three failures, high praise must attach to the effort of the chivalrous Louis de Bougainville. During the Seven Years' War he had struggled gallantly, under the leadership of Montcalm, to avert the doom of Canada, which they both foresaw; and now the junior joined the French Navy in order to restore the fortunes of France by means of the maritime discoveries suggested by de Brosses. If his nautical experience had been equal to his spirit, if also his programme had prescribed a more southerly course, he might have anticipated Cook. But in both respects he was less well prepared. The contrasts between their expeditions are full of interest.

Bougainville set sail in November, 1766, three months after Wallis, with a new frigate, *Boudeuse* (26), and a storeship, *Étoile* (20). (It was a mistake to send frigates so heavily gunned.) The Government sent with him two scientists—the first time that science was fitly

[3] The so-called Manila Galleon plied its lonesome course across the Pacific for some 250 years, carrying silver from Acapulco on the west coast of Mexico to Manila, where it picked up silks and other rich return cargo at that entrepot for Chinese goods. Except for Guam in the Marianas, it touched at almost no islands en route.

[4] The grandfather of the poet, known as Foul Weather Jack because he encountered more than a normal share of bad storms.

[5] When Francis Drake, the English "Sea Dog" visited California in 1579, on the second voyage of circumnavigation, he named it New Albion.

represented in oceanic voyages. His orders were to proceed by the south of South America, then make for the tropics, and, within the tropics, proceed towards the East Indies. His preliminary attempt at settling part of the Falkland Isles (already considered an excellent base for Pacific discoveries) had meanwhile failed; for Spain asserted her over-lordship of that group. After long delays he entered the Straits of Magellan and took fifty-two days to pass through them—a long passage, performed against strong head winds. The Pacific, however, was true to its name, and, after a fruitless search for the Southern Continent, the two ships made Tahiti, where Wallis had been eight months before. The Frenchmen admired greatly the Tahitian men and still more their women—"Whose appearance ravished the eye and the heart, and all their gestures were harmonious." Indeed, Bougainville, classical scholar as he was, now dedicated the island to Venus by naming it The New Cythera; also, disregarding the act of annexation to England, he declared it subject to France (she acquired it in 1843). The natives celebrated the new connection by offering presents, even including their wives and daughters, while they themselves stole everything of value with incredible skill.[6]

Tearing themselves away from this abode of Venus and Mercury, Bougainville next re-discovered islands which, owing to the skill of the natives in handling their lateen-sail canoes, he called The Navigators' Archipelago; we term them Samoa. Then, taking a rather more southerly course than those taken by Schouten and Tasman, he re-discovered the islands which Quiros had dedicated to the Holy Spirit, and which Cook in his second voyage was to re-name the New Hebrides. Bougain-ville, who knew Quiros's description of the islands, believed them to be the lands discovered by that idealist Spaniard.[7]

Thereafter, despite the shortness of his stock of provisions, the French voyager resolved to discover the east of New Holland by sailing due west along latitude 15°, not north-west as most voyagers had done; but after many days he met with a line of shoals and rocks, on which breakers beat with great violence. (It is still termed Bougain-ville Reef.) So he put about to the north, thus avoiding the Great Barrier Reef which proved nearly fatal to Cook three years later. Turn-ing north-east, Bougainville soon sighted a maze of islets off the south-

[6] Wallis' crew had also had a very good time in the "Amorous Isles." In fact, when Cook's crew contracted venereal disease at Tahiti in 1769, there was a question whether the sailors of Wallis in 1767 or Bougainville in 1768 were responsible.

[7] The Spaniard, Pedro de Quiros, around 1600 made two important Pacific expeditions, on the second of which he discovered the New Hebrides, where the principal settlement preserving the original Quiros name, Espiritu Santo, was an important American naval base in World War II.

eastern tip of New Guinea. If only he had known for certain that Prado and Torres had sailed on westwards, i.e. on the south side of that great island, he might have re-discovered the long forgotten Torres Straits.[8] But he deemed their existence at best highly uncertain. As he wrote in his *Journal*—"We even thought we saw the land stretch west-south-west. We had to try to get out as quickly as possible from this gulf into which we had ventured." Accordingly, he stood away to the east to get away from the endless shoals and islets, the risks from which were doubled by currents and mists. Worst of all, his crews were weak and discontented from lack of food; for he had been unable to get supplies from Quiros's islands. Also his ships, especially the smaller, worked badly, so that he could not entrust her with inshore work or exploring ahead, as might otherwise have been helpful. Indeed, in the mists they could scarcely keep in touch. So Cook was better off with one strong sound capacious ship, which he was careful to provision at all possible places, than Bougainville with two that were ill-matched. True, the French crews never underwent the awful experiences of the *Endeavour* on an isolated coral reef: but after 10th June they encountered daily risks, often in thick weather, off the long line of islets and rocks south-east of New Guinea, which he named the Louisiade Archipelago. At last on the 20th, when almost in despair, they sighted its lofty eastern tip fronting open and deep water, and, on rounding it, he gave the name Cape Deliverance. Thus, he escaped from terrible dangers, but he had missed Torres Strait. Bearing northwards, he at length hove in sight of the outlying islands belonging to that Solomon group which had eluded the search of several explorers. The most northerly one is still called after him. Finding the natives hostile, he made for Dampier's much belauded New Britain, and one of the French sailors stumbled on a lead plate with English words on it, a relic of Carteret's voyage.

Little else of interest was found in New Britain, and storms of rain weakened and discouraged the men. In fact Bougainville struck the island on the worse side, where snakes and scorpions abounded and food was lacking. So, sailing on to the west, he left New Britain unexplored. Coasting the north of New Guinea, the two ships passed through *Le Passage des Français,* and on 28th September, neared Batavia, where the Dutch tried to appease their gargantuan hunger.[9]

[8] The Spaniard Luis Vaez de Torres became separated from Quiros after discovering the New Hebrides (Espiritu Santo), and sailing northward along the Great Barrier Reef, discovered the strait between Australia and New Guinea that still bears his name, but did not recognize Australia as such.

[9] Batavia, on Java, now restored to its original name of Jakarta, was the capital of the extensive and highly profitable Dutch colonial empire, now Indonesia.

The officials, however, though piling on the food, kept all knowledge of the routes secret. Finally, with some difficulty owing to Java fever, Bougainville early in 1769 reached Cape Town, and, overtaking Carteret's *Swallow,* cast anchor in St. Malo on 16th March, 1769.

His circumnavigation, though highly creditable to a former soldier, had not achieved complete success, mainly owing to his inexperience at sea, the defects of his ships, and inability to secure or store sufficient provisions for the long crisis off New Guinea. He had re-discovered much but discovered comparatively little, and his charts were often left vague. "I think a passage may be there" occurs once or twice. (Cook would have sailed into it.) They were criticised by his greater, though tragically unfortunate, successor, La Pérouse.[10] Nevertheless, his home-coming encouraged the French to improve their navy and go on with explorations, in which the next King, Louis XVI, took great interest, for the great hobby of that crowned misfit was geography.

Bougainville's [11] chief influence lay in the political sphere; for his notes on the Dutch stations in the Far East revealed their weakness. "To desire (he wrote) the destruction of this exclusive [Dutch] trade would be to effect it. The best safeguard of the Dutch consists in the ignorance of the rest of Europe concerning the state of these isles (i.e. the Spice Islands)." Thus he quickened the desire of the French to control or conquer Holland, so as to absorb the wealth of the Far East—a fact which explains much in the actions of the French towards the Dutch Republic under Louis XVI and Napoleon. To control or annex that State would also dower France with a vast colonial empire, including world points like the Cape, Ceylon, Java and Guiana, all of which were at stake in the Napoleonic War.

Meanwhile, with admirable tenacity, in spite of the failures of 1764–68, the British Admiralty was prosecuting its plan of clearing up the problem of the Great South Land. Indeed, those failures may have suggested to some of its officials the need of taking a more southerly course in the Pacific. Also an opportunity for a new effort was afforded by the Royal Society requesting its aid for observing the transit of Venus at Tahiti in June, 1769. This occasion was long believed to be

[10] Jean de La Pérouse led a French expedition that made some very important Pacific discoveries between 1785 and 1788, ranging from Japan and Kamchatka down to Australia, where he reached the infant settlement of Sydney only a few days after the British had established their convict settlement there. He sailed away and was never heard from again; years later the wrecks of his ships were found on a wild island far to the northward.

[11] Bougainville, like La Pérouse, fought in the American Revolution; he later rose to the rank of vice-admiral. He was made a member of the leading French and British scientific societies. The beautiful flowering shrub bougainvillea was named for him.

the sole cause of the third British expedition to the Pacific, that of James Cook. But in recent years his additional secret Instructions were found by the Admiralty Librarian, the late Mr. W. G. Perrin. They show that this astronomical event was merely the pretext for a far-reaching effort at discovering *Terra Australis incognita*. In fact if the Royal Society had had its way, the commander of the expedition would have been Alexander Dalrymple, who (as we have seen) had of late been compiling a book, *Discoveries in the South Pacific*. He had strong claims, but stretched them too far by requiring to be placed in supreme command, a step incompatible with Admiralty rules. Fortunately, in this case the requirements of officialism and efficiency coincided; for the choice of My Lords fell on the ablest and best-trained of all coastal explorers.

Cook's First Voyage, 1768–1771

James Cook had long been inured to hardships both on land and sea. The son of an agricultural labourer of Marton in North Yorkshire, he from childhood knew how to fend for himself. Afterwards, both as common seaman and mate, he learnt seafaring in the Whitby coasting trade, and finally in the Royal Navy. His fine physique (he was over 6 feet), quiet but resolute behaviour and keen vision soon brought promotion during the Seven Years' War; and as "master" he rendered yeoman service in surveying with minute care the almost unknown channel of the St. Lawrence for Wolfe's famous expedition. Thereafter he was long employed in dangerous surveying work on the coasts of Newfoundland and Labrador, which he charted with his usual thoroughness, eagerly studying mathematics in his spare time in winter at Halifax so as to master the science of navigation. Thus, although he had risen from the ranks, the Admiralty (greatly to its credit) now gave him, in his fortieth year, a commission as lieutenant to command the expedition destined for the discovery of the Great Southern Continent. Dalrymple deeply resented this appointment, but generously helped the botanist of the expedition, (Sir) Joseph Banks, with information and gave him a copy of his new book, though it was not published until after Bougainville's return home in March, 1769.

Fortunately, the Admiralty allowed Cook to choose his own ship. He chose a stoutly built capacious Whitby collier, of 366 tons, which, when bought into the Royal Navy, was styled H.M. Barque *Endeavour*. She was the best and most seaworthy craft ever sent on such a quest; and the crew were as good as the ship. No smaller consort was sent for inshore work. On the other hand, the secret Instructions of 30th July,

1768, drawn up for Cook by the Admiralty, far excelled all previous programmes for Pacific exploration. They show that the chief aims of the expedition were not only geographical but political. After the astronomical duties at Tahiti were finished, Cook was to sail southward as far as latitude 40° for the purpose of discovering the great Continent which was believed to exist thereabouts. Or, if he sighted no land, he might sail westward between latitudes 35° and 40° until he found either the Continent itself or else New Zealand. He was to explore as much as possible of the new Continent, observe the ways of the natives, trade with them, gain their friendship, and, "with their consent," annex suitable parts to Great Britain. The same instructions would apply to New Zealand; and thereafter he was free to sail to "some known port, where you may procure a sufficiency (of provisions) to carry you to England, either round the Cape of Good Hope or Cape Horn, as from circumstances you may judge the most eligible way of returning home."

These Instructions were signed by the Lords of the Admiralty, Admirals Hawke and Peircy Brett, and Lord Charles Spencer. Probably Brett, who had sailed round the world with Anson in H.M.S. *Centurion*, was the chief inspirer of them, and, if so, his was the plan which led to the re-discovery of New Zealand and the discovery of Australia on the east side. Certainly Cook did not inspire them; for he knew only northern waters. The expedition was to be helped also by two astronomers, an artist, the botanists, (Sir) Joseph Banks and a Swede, Dr. Solander. Thanks to Cook's forethought in laying in good store of food, including anti-scorbutics like lemons, oranges, raisins and "sourkrout," scurvy was kept at bay. On Tierra del Fuego they gathered wild celery and mixed it with soup: so (wrote the ship's surgeon, Perry), "We passed Cape Horn, all our men as free from scurvy as on leaving Plymouth." Thus, at last, after 3000 years of seafaring and generally ill-prepared exploring, an expedition had set forth under the most favourable auspices; for it was headed by an able and thoroughly trained seaman and hydrographer, with a first-class ship and crew, and it proceeded on a well thought out quest. No contrast is more marked than that offered by Anson's *Voyage round the World* (1740–44). His sixty-gun ship, *Centurion*, was overgunned and overcrowded with weak old men. She nearly foundered in the winter gales off Cape Horn, and afterwards his 500 men were "reduced to 213," many of these weak with scurvy; and by the time they reached Juan Fernandez only ten men in a watch were fit for duty.

On the other hand, Cook experienced favourable weather round Cape Horn, and proved that in average conditions in summer, the open sea route was better than the mazy straits. His quick passage almost direct towards Tahiti disconcerted the Spaniards, whose recent fortification of the only good bay in Juan Fernandez, was intended to exclude "interlopers" from the Pacific. Cook, like Drake, helped to throw that ocean open to the world. After a quick run of only 260 days from Plymouth, he anchored at Tahiti on 11th April, 1769.

There he had abundance of time to satisfy his curiosity about the natives, whom he ordered to be treated humanely, even when they stole every possible object. He and the scientists studied carefully both them and their island, so that this sojourn of 93 days yielded more definite results for astronomy, ethnology, botany, and geology, than any voyage yet recorded. On 3rd June the transit of Venus was observed; but that goddess was in the ascendant at Tahiti; and the crew were so much weakened by their debaucheries in the island that Cook decided not to sail due south but to make first for islands only two days' sail to the west of Tahiti. This and other news Cook had from Tupia, a priest, who, being accused of murder, found it desirable to leave the island and therefore joined Cook. Tupia knew the positions of seventy-four islands, and was useful to the expedition in many ways.

Proceeding westwards from Tahiti on 13th July, Cook soon discovered four beautiful islands, which he named the Society Islands, after the Royal Society. He charted the whole group, in many parts fringed with coral reefs, and bartered with the natives for hogs and fruit. A month having been spent there in exploring and in restoring the strength of his crew, the *Endeavour* stood away southwards for other small islands with which Tupia was well acquainted, though he had never heard of any great land to the south—a fact which increased Cook's disbelief in a Southern Continent. Herein he differed from de Brosses and Dalrymple, though he frequently consulted their books.

Nevertheless, as in duty bound, he explored the sea even to the far south. Grimly he held on for many days, though the crew shivered and the Society Islands' hogs died apace. On 2nd September, when about lattitude 40°, as there was no sign of land, and cold storms beset them, he resolved to put about northwards lest the ship be too much battered. But he had gone more than 1200 miles southwards in search of what he believed to be a chimera. His scepticism was natural enough, for de Brosses and Dalrymple had maintained that the great Continent stretched over a vast area as far north as Tahiti and for thousands of miles east and west of it. And now, during many days, Cook had been sailing through it. Standing back to the north, and then in the main south-west, he at last had his reward.

On 7th October, 1769, he sighted high land to the west, in latitude 38° 57′. Was this the Great South Land? It might well be, for, as they stood into a bay (still called Poverty Bay, as Cook named it) they saw several canoes, people on the shore, buildings behind, and at the back of all high mountains, "cloathed with wood and verdure." [12] Cook's first meeting with the Maori was, however, unfortunate. He made the mistake of going ashore with too few men, and also left a boat, with four boys in, almost unguarded. This the "Indians," as he calls them, were about to seize, and carry off the boys, had not muskets been fired, killing one of the assailants. Next day Cook brought on shore more men, and Tupia spoke to the natives soothingly in Tahitian, which they quite understood; but nothing would stop their rapacity until musketry killed one and wounded three more.

Leaving this "Poverty Bay," Cook coasted along southwards, meeting generally with defiance and hostility. In part of Hawke's Bay (which he thus named after the First Lord, Admiral Hawke) bartering went on at the ship's side until one canoe's crew sought to carry off Tupia's native boy, and would have done so had not two of the cannibals been killed by musket shots. Hence the name "Kidnappers Cape." Finding the people to the south equally hostile and the coast unpromising, he put about at "Cape Turnagain" (latitude 40° 34′ S.) and sailed northwards. In the warmer districts farther north he found the Maori less fierce and ready to trade, offering their yams and sweet potatoes, even the paddles of their canoes, for hatchets and big nails (they had never seen iron before, being in the Stone Age).

In a great bay and river (the Thames) Banks admired "the finest timber I ever beheld"; and in this district he and Solander could botanise without danger from the natives, who were very different from the fierce cannibals of Poverty Bay and Hawke's Bay. After a stay in the glorious Bay of Islands, Cook at last sighted the northern tip of the land, and there (like Tasman 127 years before) he noted in rough weather "the large swell rowling in from the west" which denoted open sea in that quarter. Hereabouts he passed near, but did not sight, a French trading ship commanded by de Surville. Then, coasting southwards along the dangerous lee shore and past the giant sugar loaf mountain ("Mount Egmont"), he entered a great bay where the strong current at length warned him that he must be in a strait. It was so; and it is fitly named Cook Strait. After passing through it, he turned to the north-east until he saw the outline of 'Cape Turnagain," and thus, after four months' sailing, proved that what he had circumnavigated was a great island, now called the "North Island" of New Zealand.

After refreshing his crew in a sheltered fiord, Queen Charlotte Sound, he set about exploring the shores to the south, surveying them

---

[12] This was New Zealand, previously discovered and named by Tasman.

with the minute care which makes his coastal map of New Zealand still valuable. There were only two serious errors. The first was in thinking Banks' Peninsula an island; but this error was due to his there putting far out to the south-east in search of land which his lieutenant, Gore, stoutly maintained was there, whereas it was only a bank of clouds; consequently Cook believed the projecting Banks' Peninsula to be an island. The second mistake was due to bad weather; for, at the extremity of what is now called "South Island," mists and variable winds compelled him to stand out from what he believed to be a bay, though it is really a strait separating South Island from Stewart Island. High westerly winds also prevented a full examination of Dusky Bay or of the ironbound coast further north, until, on the forty-sixth day he reentered Cook Strait and thus proved that New Zealand consisted of two large islands with a coast line of over 2000 miles—another blow (as Banks noted) to the theory of a great southern continent. But he had found the finest home for the white race yet discovered by any explorer of the southern hemisphere; and that, too, in spite of the description of the Maori by Parkinson, Bank's draughtsman, as "cannibals, accustomed to the carnage of war from infancy, and peculiarly undaunted," while those of the South Island were "a set of poor mean wretches, who . . . want the spirit or sprightliness of those of the North Island. . . . Their canoes are but mean."

In Queen Charlotte Sound Cook again laid in provisions and had to face the problem—where to find that elusive Continent. In his Journal of 31st March, 1770, he records his desire to return homwards by an immense sweep to the south-east in high latitudes towards Cape Horn. But to do so would be to brave the coming Antarctic winter, with a crew now wearied, and a ship battered by gales—risks which even Cook counted too great; for his zeal was always tempered by prudence, the fruit of long experience. Neither could he undertake without grave danger a long sweep in a south-westerly direction, against the prevalent winds, into the far south of the Indian Ocean and back to England by the Cape of Good Hope. Therefore, after consulting his officers, he decided to take an alternative course allowed him by his secret Instructions, and sail for the east coast of New Holland, follow it to the North and try to "fall in with the land or islands discovered by Quiros." Here, truly, was a safe but still an attractive alternative. Cook knew not that it would lead him towards the "isle of continent" on its most fertile side. And once more we note that the Admiralty, in prescribing a search in the far south-west of the Pacific, opened up this glorious prospect.

Again Cook proved to be an ideal executant of its plans. On 19th

April, 1770, after a nineteen days' run from Cape Farewell, he sighted at Point Hicks in latitude 37° 58' the south-east of a land which he reckoned to be not far from the east coast of Van Diemen's Land.[13] Had he not been driven north by a hard southerly gale on the previous day, he might have run into the great bight which we know as Bass Strait. By this piece of bad luck his landfall was near the south-east end of the province of Victoria. Even so, he concluded, "from the soon falling of the sea after the wind abated," that there was land to the south-west, and he doubted whether the coast now sighted joined on to Van Diemen's Land. Thus, as his object was to coast northwards up any land that he might find, he proceeded to the north-east past Cape Howe and a shore, "which had a very agreeable and promising aspect, diversified with hills, ridges, plains and valleys." In this verdict, Banks and he agreed. So this was the first time that white men had anything good to say about Australia, for all their predecessors had struck that land on its weather-beaten, almost barren sides of the west and north-west. Thanks to the forethought shown in the Admiralty secret Instructions, Cook approached both New Zealand and Australia on their eastern and as yet unexplored coasts. Both Banks and he were hopeful as to the fertility of this new land. But on 29th April, when they entered a bay further north, Cook called it in his log Sting-Ray Harbour. Only in a later chart does it appear as "Botany Bay." But Parkinson gave a better verdict about that inlet. He described the shore as fertile and abounding in flowering shrubs so that "from the number of curious plants we met with we called the bay Botany Bay." He, then, seems to be the author of that much disputed name.

Cook's full description of that bay and of the long eastern coast line cannot even be summarised here. The accuracy of his survey may be seen by comparing his chart of 1770 with the surveys carried out up to 1890. Cook's work is at fault only as regards secluded inlets, like Port Jackson, which he had no time to enter. Off that glorious but almost hidden harbour he wrote in his Journal, Sunday, 8th May, 1770:— "About two or three miles from the land abreast of a bay, wherein there appeared to be a safe anchorage, and which I called Port Jackson." Like a careful seaman Cook sailed some three or more miles out from that unknown shore, and further out still as he proceeded along the jagged coast of what we call Queensland. He was nearing the inner fringe of the Great Barrier Reef, the mightiest and most dangerous in the world.

Cook had sailed more than half round the globe without encountering grave peril. He had shown himself a highly skilled navigator and ex-

[13] Now Tasmania.

plorer, equable in temper, sound in judgment, careful of the health of his crew, beloved by them and by the natives whom he studied with sympathetic zeal, unrivalled at charting coasts, and a correct chronicler of events, which he later described in a convincing narrative. But it is in deadly danger that the great seaman stands forth supreme. Off Cape Tribulation (lat. 16°) on 11th June, signs of rocks and of shallowing water had led Cook, early on a fine moonlight night, to stand on through a deeper stretch under easy sail, when, of a sudden, the *Endeavour* struck fast on the tail of a coral reef. At once he ordered sails to be taken in and boats lowered to examine her position. She lay pierced by a rock in a hollow of the reef, motionless but for the heavy beating of the ocean swell, which soon carried away her false keel. Destruction seeming imminent, Cook ordered six guns, casks of stores, ballast, etc., to be heaved overboard, also anchors to be carried out to windward to steady the ship.

So passed that awful night, with incessant toil at the pumps; for the *Endeavour* heeled over and leaked badly with ebb tide; but what would happen at next high tide (11 A.M.) if the breeze freshened? Dawn showed the nearest land eight leagues distant; but now the breeze died away and the sea calmed. With the flood tide, however, the ship righted herself and widened the leak; so the water poured in and defied their efforts at three pumps. Nevertheless, Cook, resourceful as ever, ordered the jettison of everything that could be spared, and then sent off a boat to carry out astern a ship's anchor with a cable, which the crew then hauled in by the windlass, so as "to heave her off the rock." This daring plan of his succeeded at 10:20 A.M., when the rising tide and the tug of the rope dragged her off the reef into deep water. Again there was an agonising struggle with the pumps against the leak, all on board taking their turn at the pumps fifteen minutes a time; but Cook resolved to "fother the ship by a sail," which was clogged with oakum and then carried out ahead by a boat's crew and thrust under the bows to the leak. By this device the inrush of water was checked and soon one pump alone kept the leak under. A landward breeze rising, they hoisted more sail, and at nightfall anchored well off the coast. On the morrow they made for an estuary which their pinnace had discovered two leagues away. There, in the mouth of the Endeavour River, where Cooktown now stands, they began the long toil of repairing their almost shattered barque, and found that the chief fracture was still almost closed by the piece of coral rock which had pierced it. They owed their preservation partly to this providential circumstance, partly to favourable weather, but equally to the unfailing resourcefulness of Cook. Under his calm but energetic control the devoted crew worked (says Banks) with unruffled courage and with a remarkable absence of oaths.

During their stay in that river (15th June—4th August) they saw several natives, who were whenever possible thievish, though Parkinson described them as "merry and facetious," and having canoes with out-riggers—an advance, due doubtless to contact with the Papuans. But one party of four came alongside in a small canoe, ten feet long, and propelled by poles, obviously only for use in shallows. As for the fauna, they marvelled at a creature "that bounded forward on two legs instead of running on four." But it provided tasty food, which, together with that of goats, wolves, birds, polecats, fish, turtle and shell fish, restored them all to full strength and supplied the provisions that Bougainville's crews lacked before their long trials off that coast.

Well was it for Cook, as later for Bligh, that their crews were refreshed before tackling the perils of the Barrier Reef and Torres Strait. Those of the mighty reef were appalling. Cook describes it as "a wall of coral rock rising almost perpendicular out of the unfathomable ocean, always overflown at high water,—generally seven or eight feet—and dry in places at low water," on which the ocean billows broke mountains high. Again, on 17th August, after rushing inside through a fearsomely narrow gap, he writes:—"It is but a few days ago that I rejoiced at having got without the reef: but that joy was nothing compared to what I now felt at being safe at anchor within it." Yet he had to struggle on with all speed towards Batavia; for the south-east Trade Wind which now helped him northward, would in November change to north-west, and thus prevent his reaching that port, the nearest place for thorough repairs to his patched up ship.

Cook believed "that this land did not join to New Guinea. But this I hope soon to prove or disprove. The islands discovered by Quiros lies (sic) in this parallel, but how far to the eastward it's hard to say. We are morally certain that he never was upon this coast." Neverthe-less, Cook kept the *Endeavour* skirting this dangerous shore in order to prove whether or no it joined New Guinea. For, though Cook knew of Dalrymple's arguments as to the existence of Torres Strait, he doubted as to their soundness. The only way to reach certainty was to sail through it. Great therefore was his joy on reaching the northern end of this perilous coast. At the tip, which he named Cape York after the late Duke of York, brother of George III, he landed (21st August, 1770), hoisted English colours and took possession of the whole shore line of some 2000 miles which he had discovered. Further west he had less interest in the coast because Dutch seaman had explored it. Moreover, to thread his way through the rockstrewn waters ahead with a leaking ship and a weary crew, taxed all their powers. But he now saw those waters to be a strait, "which until this day hath been a doubtful point with geographers."

After landing in the south of New Guinea (3rd September) near Triton Bank, i.e. far to the west of Torres Strait, he noted in his Journal that he had seen in maps published in de Brosses' *Voyages to the Terra Australis* (1756) that—"the Spaniards and Dutch have at one time or another circumnavigated New Guinea." But that author did not name Torres, and evidently regarded the existence of a strait on the south of New Guinea as hitherto debatable. We are therefore justified in saying that the work of Torres and Prado had been forgotten; and that, for all practical purposes, Cook made known the strait to the world. He had rendered an even greater service by revealing the dangers of the Barrier Reef, thereby warning off future explorers from what was a gigantic death trap. Indeed, unlike most of his predecessors, he worked for all the world, and his detailed and accurate charts must have saved thousands of lives. National jealousies now began, though slowly, to be replaced by mutual aid, to the great gain of navigation.

The stay at Batavia for repairs was marked by a heavy mortality, only twenty of the crew being fit for duty; among the losses by death were Tupia and his boy. After a time of rest in Table Bay (which he much admired) he made for home, and on 13th July, 1771, landed in the Downs and proceeded to London. In a postscript to his Journal he proved his originality by drafting a new and comprehensive plan of explorations, such as was impossible in 1769, when he was merely an executant of Admiralty policy. He now pointed out that the best way of exploring the Pacific Ocean would be by way of the Cape of Good Hope, thence to the south of New Holland, thence to Queen Charlotte Sound for refreshment, leaving it by the end of September or early October, so as to have the whole summer for searching the South Pacific in high latitudes for the supposed continent; or, in case of failure, turn to the north and proceed with the Trade Wind to the west in search of islands:—"thus the discoveries in the South Sea would be complete."

Cook's Second Voyage, 1772–1775

The modesty of the great explorer appears strikingly in this postscript, which was probably written after Dalrymple and other champions of a great Southern Continent had tried to belittle Cook's achievement. In reality by sailing down far south in the mid-Pacific, by circumnavigating New Zealand and coasting along the east of New Holland, he had disproved the existence of any vast tract of land in the temperate zone. Still, as French explorers were active, and the Admiralty wished him to clear up that problem, he consented (now with the rank of commander) to lead an expedition of two Whitby-built ships, the *Resolution* (463 tons) and the *Adventure* (336 tons) which were equipped with the utmost care for the health of the crews. The Admiralty accepted his advice to sail by way of the Cape of Good Hope and New Zealand. After leaving Cape Town he put far to the south in the hope of sighting Cape Circumcision which the French explorer, Bouvet, had named in 1739, in the belief that it formed the north point of the Southern Continent. (It is a worthless islet surrounded by watery wastes.) Cook did not find it. Much farther to the west he crossed the Antarctic Circle—a feat never before accomplished, but during 117 days he was out of sight of land and often in danger from icebergs and the ice-pack.

After refreshing his weary crew in New Zealand, first in Dusky Bay and then in Queen Charlotte Sound, where he met the *Adventure* again, he proceeded east and south-east in search of Dalrymple's Southern Continent, but found only open waters with the "large hollow swell" of the ocean. At last, after being driven north to Tahiti by continued hardships which (says Forster, a German scientist on board) had reduced him almost to a skeleton, he returned to Queen Charlotte Sound to restore his crew to health (the *Adventure* by this time having separated in storms). Then again he assailed the southern waste of waters, once stretching as far south as 71° 10′—the farthest south of any white man. Again worn to the bone by privations and severe cold, he had to turn north and finally sighted Easter Island, where they marvelled at the gigantic statues. Thence voyaging westwards Cook thoroughly explored the New Hebrides (as he named them), and next discovered New Caledonia and Norfolk Island: the New Scots he found to be both friendly and honest. He then returned to New Zealand for a time of rest in his favourite sound—his advanced base for Pacific explorations. For the third time he sailed forth to find that elusive continent, far to the south of and beyond Cape Horn. Again he failed, but only because nothing was attainable in habitable latitudes. Yet on his homeward voyage he surveyed the south-west coast of Tierra del Fuego, especially Cook Bay, west of the Beagle Channel. There he anchored in Christmas Sound. Rounding Cape Horn on 29th December, 1774, he next re-discovered, in the South Atlantic, South Georgia, and discovered the Sandwich Group about latitude 59° S. and longitude 28° W.—both of them being in the midst of Dalrymple's Great South Land. He then expressed the belief that there must be a large tract of land near the South Pole, owing to the many islands, the excessive cold and the vast floats of ice encountered in the far South—a surmise equally shrewd and correct. Quitting this "poor apology for a Continent," he made for the Cape and then England, which the *Resolution* reached without the loss of a topmast during more than three years.

Does not the world owe him eternal gratitude for heroic perseverance with a programme which he believed to be illusory? Has any man ever worked so long and desperately to dispel the illusion of a great, populous and wealthy southern continent? Surely never. All friends of peace must hail his memory as that of a man who exploded what was a baneful legend, breeding jealousy among the European nations. Finally, all friends of sailors must admire his unceasing care for the health of his crew, especially by his intelligent use of that advanced base, Queen Charlotte Sound, which enabled him thrice to defy the rigours of the Antarctic, and yet, during those long and very trying efforts, lose by illness only one man out of 118—a striking contrast to Vasco da Gama's loss of 115 out of 170 from four ships in his voyage to and from Calicut (1497–99). Richly, then, did Cook deserve the Fellowship of the Royal Society awarded to him early in 1776.

Cook's Third Voyage, 1776–1779

In his third voyage (1776–79) Cook (now at last captain) measured his skill and strength against that most baffling of problems, the North-West Passage. This quest had gripped the attention of far-seeing merchants of Bristol and London ever since the year 1527, when their spokesman, Robert Thorne, begged Henry VIII to discover "the short way to the Spicery by our Seas" and "in the backe side of the New Found Land." Obviously England would benefit by the discovery of such a route; and from the time of the Cabots strenuous efforts had been made to find that short cut to Japan, China and the Spice Islands. On this alluring but delusive quest, Frobisher and other English sailors ventured far into polar seas with myriad hardships and no result. The first to suggest an attempt from the Pacific to the Atlantic was Drake, who, when off New Albion, proposed to explore "what passage there was to be found from the South Sea into our own Ocean," abut latitude 66° N.—a singularly good guess at the eastern exit. But finally he was deterred by the deepening cold and fogs. Dampier had the same vision; but his pals preferred the run to the Spice Islands.

Not until the voyages of Bering (1728–41) was the legendary "Anian" strait between Asia and North America discovered. He, a Dane in the Russian service, completed the Russian discoveries of

Kamchatka, struggled through the strait named after him and caught glimpses of Alaska. But he had to put back and encountered hardships and disease which led to his death and that of thirty others by scurvy on one of the Aleutian Islands. These terrible experiences emphasised the need of finding further south a channel connecting the Atlantic and Pacific Oceans. For the idea still persisted that there must be such a passage; and hopes had long centred in Hudson Bay. When, in 1713, the Peace of Utrecht placed Great Britain securely in possession of that bay, expeditions set forth to explore the west coast of that vast inland sea. In 1719 certain merchants sent out Captain Barlow to find the short route to China. He and his crew were never heard of again, though in 1748 the wreckage of his ship was found in the bay. In 1722 Captain Scroggs reached latitude 64° 56' and, there, mounting a head-land, sighted a channel to the south-west, whereupon he tamely re-turned. In 1741–42, Captain Middleton made repeated efforts to find a western passage, but in vain. Nevertheless, in 1745 Parliament voted a prize of £20,000 "to the owner or his assigns" of a ship that should discover, and *sail through* a passage to the Pacific; but seamen apparently regarded the offer, with that cautious proviso, as an official joke.

Meanwhile Russians from Alaska were working southwards, and Spaniards from California northwards; but nothing much resulted except trade with the Indians and the prospect of a struggle between those two Powers for that great coast-line. In 1765 Byron neglected his orders to try and find a strait through to Hudson Bay. In 1774 the Spaniard Perez explored parts of the west coast up to latitude 55°, and in 1775 Quadra reached 56°.[14] At last, in 1776, Great Britain made a bid for the shores of what is now British Columbia. Thus, in the year which witnessed the beginning of the disruption of the Empire, occurred also an event which opened up a new avenue for expansion.

Following Cook's advice always to sail via the Cape of Good Hope for the exploration of the Pacific, the Admiralty issued secret Instructions (July, 1776) that he should proceed by that route for the "search of a North-East or North-West Passage from the Pacific Ocean into the Atlantic Ocean or the North Sea." Again, then, he was allowed wide latitude so long as he avoided contact with any Spanish settlement in the Pacific, a rupture with Spain being then not unlikely. He was to coast along New Albion as far as latitude 65° N., and thereabouts very carefully search for and explore all considerable rivers or inlets "pointing towards Hudson's or Baffin's Bays"—a proof of the utter uncertainty still hanging over the North-West. The recent efforts of

[14] This movement north from California was the last burst of energy on the part of the old Spanish Empire.

Samuel Hearne to find by land "a new passage into the South Sea" had in 1771 taken him down the Coppermine River to the Arctic Ocean and thence back to the Great Slave Lake. Yet somehow (perhaps owing to the legendary cruise of de Fuca soon to be noted), the hope persisted that there might be such a passage about, or north of, latitude 65°; and the reward of £20,000 offered in 1745 for such a discovery was now renewed.

It was a forlorn hope; yet even so, Cook accomplished marvels with H.M.S. *Resolution* and *Discovery*. For his bold plan of sailing across the Pacific from New Zealand to New Albion struck right athwart the well-beaten track of Magellan, which had yielded very few discoveries. His reward was the discovery of Christmas Island and next the Sandwich (Hawaiian) Islands (January, 1778).[15] His claim to have discovered the latter group has been denied on the claim that a Spaniard, Juan Gaëtano, had sighted those islands in 1555. This claim is doubtful; and a recent examination of the evidence by Bishop Resterick of Hawaii seems to disprove it. Certainly at that time the Spaniards knew nothing whatever about these islands.

Cook was "agreeably surprised to find that the Hawaiians spoke the language of Otaheite (Tahiti) and of the other islands we had lately visited." Indeed in his three voyages he was the first to prove and record the extraordinary fact that the Polynesians had spread all over the Pacific "from New Zealand in the South to the Sandwich Islands in the North, and from Easter Island to the New Hebrides, i.e., over 60° of latitude and over 83° of longitude: . . . certainly it is the most extensive nation upon earth." The statement illustrates his exact observation and powers of reasoning. Further, his careful study of those peoples—their tools, weapons, canoes and customs—entitles him to a very high place among Pacific ethnologists.

In kindliness, keen curiosity and expert thieving the Hawaiians resembled other Polynesians; but, unlike the Maoris in 1769, they fell flat on their faces when Cook landed, as before a god, and they offered gifts, especially pigs, to "Orono." During the fortnight there his relations with the islanders were fairly cordial in spite of much thieving; and by barter his two ships procured so large a stock of provisions and fruit as to arouse pity for Anson and his famishing crew who knew not of the existence of these large and fertile islands not far from his track. Cook's discoveries now robbed the centre of the Pacific Ocean

[15] Cook, with "his finger on his number," as the navy says, named the islands for the Earl of Sandwich, First Lord of Admiralty, the reputed inventor of the sandwich, who is said to have done more damage to the Navy than any hostile admiral had done.

of its terrors. Indeed, he is the chief revealer of that ocean, from the Antarctic to the Arctic, from New South Wales to Alaska.

A run of thirty-three days brought Cook's ships to the shores of New Albion. Coasting along northwards, he encountered adverse winds and boisterous weather, which, driving them out to sea, probably accounts for his missing the entrance to Juan de Fuca Strait—one of the very few important misses of his career. At last, at the end of March, he made land near a fine natural harbour, Nootka Sound. Canoes at once came out and Indian orators extended a formal welcome and offers of barter. Trade with the Spaniards had sharpened their wits, which, as in Oceania, were directed largely to the acquisition of metals either by bargaining or thieving. Cook found them docile, courteous and indolent, good-natured but quick to resent an affront. Their canoes, made of hollowed out trees, had no sails or outriggers, which (adds Cook) "distinguishes them from the Pacific islanders and the south of the East Indies." During a month's stay the Indians remained eager to barter skins and furs for metals, either iron or brass; and the trade thus happily begun was to lead to further intercourse in the future; for among his crews were Portlock, Meares, Colnett and others who noted the cheapness of furs at Nootka and the beginnings farther north of Russian trade with China. These men and others subsequently formed the King George's Sound Company and opened a promising trade with China. In 1787, Captain N. Portlock recorded that this opening encouraged a Canadian (probably Peter Pond or Alexander Mackenzie) to attempt a passage over the intervening mountains in order to extend the Canadian fur trade to the coast. So Cook's third voyage "opened to commerce several extensive prospects."

The effort of Spain in 1789 to stamp out the Nootka settlement and trade brought stiff and successful resistance from William Pitt, who sent out one of Cook's men, George Vancouver, to hoist the British flag and make discoveries. His survey of the coast of north-west America up to latitude 63° was so thorough as to prove that no North-West Passage could exist in habitable latitudes. He thus refuted the much talked of reports of the Greek pilot, de Fuca, to have sailed, about latitude 47°, into a great inland sea which brought them near to Hudson's Bay (1592–3). Vancouver also proved the insularity of the whole Nootka area, which therefore bears his name. But our first title to British Columbia was due to Cook.

Sailing away from Nootka Sound on 26th April, 1778, towards the north-west, he encountered a hurricane which swept him far from land, and he sighted none until he neared Capes Fairweather and Suckling.

Farther north he explored a great bay, which he named after Prince William, but it led to no channel eastwards. In latitude 59° he entered a deep gulf running to the north-east, which aroused high hopes. These hopes faded as the water became brackish and then almost fresh. "So (writes Cook) I was convinced we were in a large river, and not in a strait communicating with the northern seas. But I was desirous of stronger proofs"—a sign of the true explorer. Further struggles to the east brought him to muddy and quite fresh water; and the "master's" pinnace, exploring the northern inlet up to 61° 30′ North, reported the same disappointing results. Very fitly, however, did the Admiralty afterwards name this gulf "Cook Sound." Signs of Russian trade began to appear as they struggled round the long Alaska Peninsula and then north towards Bering's Strait. There Cook named the westernmost tip of America after the Prince of Wales. He also noted with interest the habits of the Esquimaux (as years before he had observed those of the Labrador natives) and in particular the ways in which Russian traders had in part improved and in part cowed them. As for their canoes, they resembled those of the Greenlanders, the framing being of slender laths, and the covering of seal-skins; they carried one man who sat in the round hole near the middle, but a second could lie down at the bottom. Helped sometimes by the Russians, and always by the natives, Cook struggled into the Arctic Ocean; but along the north-west coast of Alaska the difficulties from ice increased, and off Icy Cape he resolved to desist from what was, after August, an impossible quest. He now planned to winter at the Sandwich Islands, using them as an advanced base for the next attack on the North-West Passage. Alas! he met his end at the hands of those islanders (14th February, 1779).

The career of Cook is remarkable for the steady growth of faculties which make for success—constancy and fortitude learnt in early struggles, tenacity in the pursuit of well considered plans, keen and close observation both of man and of Nature, and a sound judgment that ripened with difficulties and nearly always triumphed over them. Such was the make-up of this stalwart Yorkshireman, whose quiet but firm demeanour, unfailing sincerity, mental alertness and friendly ways that rarely were marred by faults of temper, gained the respect and affection of all men, of all classes, in all lands. His rise from a humble station to the rank of captain in the Royal Navy and the honourable position of Fellow of the Royal Society was highly creditable alike to him and his country; for, though his second and third voyages aimed at the unattainable, yet he cheerfully and intelligently pursued both quests and retained throughout the loyal and unswerving support of his officers and men admidst hardships worse than those which baffled Bougainville off Papua.

Like all great men, he inspired others to carry on his work. Among his pupils were Vancouver and others who opened up North Pacific trade; also Bligh, the hero of the greatest voyage ever made in an open boat; and he in his turn trained Flinders, the first circumnavigator of Australia. Thus Cook's influence lived on in widening circles. Indeed, he attained by kindly means far more than any martinet could snatch at by harshness. . . .

His end was a mysterious tragedy; for he had ever befriended natives. Even the murderers soon lamented their deed, and asked, weeping, whether Orono would not come back. His death was a loss to them and to the world at large. For he was ever thoughtful for their welfare, and he might still have accomplished wonders in the spheres of exploration and ethnology, possessing as he did keen interest in man and Nature, unequalled experience in coastal surveys, an unflinching will in the execution of orders, and untiring patience in collecting all the relevant evidence. Accordingly, he merits the verdict placed by his widow on the memorial tablet in St. Andrew-the-Great Church, Cambridge—*Nil intentatum reliquit.* And these qualities were crowned by sound judgment. Never did he jump to a conclusion as to a prominent headland being the tip of the Southern Continent. Like a trained hydrographer he examined headland or gulf, river or reef, with all possible care. Therefore nearly all his conclusions have stood the test of time; and his charts, like his accounts of natives, are of high value even to-day.

. . . Sir Clements Markham, himself a distinguished explorer and critic of explorers, hailed him as "first in the glorious roll of maritime discoverers, not only in his own time but for all time." This panegyric is fully deserved; for Cook in his first voyage not only discovered but accurately charted more than 4000 miles of habitable coast-line; in his second he dispelled the dangerous legend of the Great South Land and revealed the true South, along with many new islands; and in his third he cleared up the mysteries of the central and north-east Pacific, besides opening up the north-west American shore to trade and future colonisation. In the handling both of ship and crew during three long and trying voyages, he stands forth a great captain; while his speedy and successful grappling with the dreadful crisis on the Barrier Reef bespeaks the consummate seaman. Further, by his keen interest in natives and their customs he excels all previous navigators. Finally, no conqueror won for mankind by long and bloody wars a tithe of the new homelands which James Cook opened up by peaceful means.

NOTES

Bern Anderson, *Surveyor of the Seas: The Life and Voyages of Captain George Vancouver*, Seattle, 1960.

C. M. Barbeau, *Pathfinders of the North Pacific*, Caldwell, Idaho, 1958.

John C. Beaglehole, *The Exploration of the Pacific*, London, 1934.

James Cook, *The Journals of Captain Cook on His Voyages of Discovery*, John C. Beaglehole et al. (eds.), 4 vols. Cambridge Eng., 1955.

Frank A. Golder, *Russian Expansion in the Pacific, 1641–1850*, Cleveland, Ohio, 1910.

Geoffrey C. Ingleton, *Charting a Continent: A Brief Memoir on the History of Marine Exploration and Hydrographical Surveying in Australian Waters*, Sydney, 1944.

Newton A. Rowe, *A Voyage to the Amorous Isles: The Discovery of Tahiti*, London, 1956.

William L. Schurz, *The Manila Galleon*, New York, 1939 (paper, 1959).

C. Andrew Sharp, *The Discovery of the Pacific Islands*, Oxford, 1960.

Joseph C. Shipman, *William Dampier, Seaman-Scientist*, Lawrence, Kansas, 1962.

THE EXPLORATION OF AFRICA *

C. E. Carrington

The history of Africa has been profoundly affected by its climate, for it has more area within the tropics than all the other continents combined. Outside that torrid zone, North Africa has been a part of the Mediterranean world since ancient times, with Europeans able to make their homes there fairly comfortably. South Africa has been an even better "white man's country," with European settlements ever since the Dutch first went there in 1652. But between the Nile cataracts and the Zambezi River, the vast areas of West Africa and East Africa have been a different matter. South of the great Sahara Desert, West Africa in particular has had a sinister reputation as the "white man's grave," thanks to excessive rainfall and steaming heat. Coupled with that, Africa's rivers, except for the lower Nile, are not

* C. E. Carrington, *The British Overseas: Exploits of a Nation of Shopkeepers* (Cambridge, England: Cambridge University Press, 1950), pp. 639–653. By permission of Cambridge University Press.

*suitable for major navigation in from the sea. Consequently the interior
of tropical Africa remained long neglected.*

At the very outset the Portuguese had eighty-odd years of close
contact with Africa, but despite the supplies of slaves and gold, this
was largely negative, because their chief concern was to find a way to
get around the continent. Once Vasco da Gama had pushed past Good
Hope to India, European interest in Africa waned. Almost the only
activity was on the Guinea Coast, where Europeans were heavily
engaged in the slave trade, and on the Barbary Coast, where North
African pirates were preying on European shipping.

The interior of the Dark Continent continued to be pretty much
a mystery. Some of the Arab slave traders penetrated inland from the
east coast in plying their nefarious business, and there were a few
pioneer explorers, particularly Mungo Park, who discovered parts of
the Niger River around 1800.

Then, in the third quarter of the nineteenth century, Livingstone,
Stanley, and a few other explorers suddenly made the world "Africa-
conscious," just as Cook and Bougainville had made it "South Sea-
conscious" a century earlier. This time, the effects were to be infinitely
more thoroughgoing. In less than two decades much of the continent
was divided up among the powers in the first great scramble of the
new imperialism.

The exploration that led to this scramble was largely by the British,
and part of the impetus came from their Royal Geographical Society.
Burton, Speke, and Baker found the upper reaches of the Nile and
discovered Lake Victoria. David Livingstone, a Scottish medical missionary, traced the course of the Zambezi and found Victoria Falls. Then
he moved up toward Lake Tanganyika, hoping to curb the slave trade.
His writings had already aroused wide public interest when he disappeared from view. An American newspaper publisher sent his prize
reporter, Henry M. Stanley, a native of Wales, out to find him. He
found Livingstone and later continued to trace the whole course of
the mighty Congo. He also wrote copiously, creating even wider interest
in the possibilities of tropical Africa. He himself went down to establish
a "Congo Free State" for King Leopold II of Belgium.

The following passage comes from one of the best accounts of
British colonial development. It devotes most of its emphasis to the
British explorers, who were the most important, anyway. But there
were some other Europeans who contributed to the revealing of African
mysteries, particularly de Brazza, du Chaillu, Nachtigal, and Schwein-
furth.

By the mid 1880's the scramble was in full swing, with Britain,

France, Germany, and Italy staking off colonial areas—France even
annexed the Sahara Desert as a matter of "map coloring" prestige.
By the end of the century, the old native empires of Ethiopia (Abys-
sinia) and Morocco, together with Liberia, established for freed Negro
slaves from America, were the only parts of Africa that had not come
under European control.

Although the whole coastline of Africa had been visited by Europeans through a period of 300 years the interior was quite unknown
to the Western nations in the eighteenth century. Neither Portuguese,
nor Dutch at the Cape, nor slave-traders of the Guinea Coast made
many attempts to penetrate the savage and unhealthy hinterland. The
system of lakes and rivers in Central Africa, which Pliny had vaguely
indicated on hearsay evidence, was no better understood 1700 years
later when Dean Swift wrote:

> So Geographers, in Afric maps,
> With savage pictures fill their gaps,
> And o'er unhabitable downs
> Place elephants for want of towns.

The Sahara and the equatorial forests alike proved fatal to European
invaders who seemed to be less resistant to tropical diseases than
Africans or Asiatics.

Yet it would be incorrect to describe Africa as undiscovered when
it was merely undiscovered by Europeans. The region of the Upper
Nile had been Christianised at least as early as the fourth century by
Copts from Egypt, whose societies were overrun and largely destroyed
by Moslem Arabs in the eleventh century. One relic of the earlier age
suvived in the kingdom of Abyssinia, embedded in Islam and lost to the
view of Western Christendom, except that some legend of its existence
continued in the fabulous tales of Prester John. The truth was revealed
by Portuguese missionaries of the sixteenth century, whose experiences
were made familiar to English readers by Samuel Johnson's translation
(1735) of Father Lobo's voyages (1626). Elsewhere the Arabs had overrun the north coast of Africa in the early days of Islam. By the eleventh
century they had spread westward from the Nile to the Niger and had
reached the ocean by way of the Senegal River. The celebrated but
mysterious city of Timbuktu was founded about A.D. 1100.

Moslem proselytism has been continuous among the negroes and
has met with no small success. Even at the present day Islam is said
to be spreading more rapidly than Christianity in Africa. The Moslem

cities of the Upper Niger region attained a high degree of civilisation and, through Islamic law and the practice of pilgrimages, preserved their contact with the Arab world. Their weakness was their addiction to slave-raiding, with the consequence that human life was held in low esteem in Central Africa. It should be remembered that the Arabs were the purveyors of the merchandise which the European slave-traders handled as middlemen.

The pagan country to the southward could also exhibit patches of characteristic civilisation. Negro kingdoms, at Dahomey, Kumasi, Benin and elsewhere, were highly developed states with formulated constitutions and sophisticated arts and crafts. They were however damned in the eyes of Europeans since they practised witchcraft and ritual murder, immolating crowds of victims as sacrifices to their divine kings. In the last days of the African slave trade these 'customs' of the West African kingdoms provided the Arab raiders with a profitable side-line in the supply of victims fro sacrifice. Perhaps both there and in East Africa the natives were sociologically decadent. It may be that the ruined cities of Rhodesia were once inhabited by negro nations at a higher stage of civilisation than the West African kingdoms but there is no agreement upon this point among the antiquaries.

Some of the first European penetrations into the interior of Africa were made by officers of the consular services, an organisation of which the history is not well known. The British consular service came unnoticed into existence in the days of the old chartered companies. The earliest consuls in the Near and Far East were the servants of the Levant and East India Companies respectively, and passed into government employment when these companies lost their privileges, in 1825 and 1858. They had no sort of political status and can hardly be said to have belonged to an official hierarchy. But John Baldwin, an orientalist, held an appointment from the Foreign Office as Consul-general in Egypt as early as 1786. Commonly they received no salary but recompensed themselves, often handsomely, by charging fees for commercial services. A series of reforms instituted by the Foreign Office, in 1856, 1876 and 1903, gradually converted the consular service into a department of government, though it was still inferior in status to the diplomatic service, a typical paradox in the English system. The nation of shopkeepers treated the agency which helped them to live and grow rich as less important than an agency largely concerned with social relations between courts and aristocracies. Yet, in the old informal days, many distinguished travellers and cosmopolitans lived abroad in ease and affluence by holding consular appointments.

James Bruce (1730–94), who was brought up in the Lisbon wine-trade, became British consul at Algiers. Thence after travelling through Egypt he made his way to Massawa in the Red Sea and, in 1769, went up-country to Gondar, the capital of Abyssinia. After exploring the headwaters of the Blue Nile, which he took to be the main source of the Great River, he returned to Europe, by way of Egypt, in 1774. His experiences in Abyssinia were received with much scepticism by stay-at-homes so that, from that time, the Nile Quest shared with the search for the North-west Passage the reputation of being an almost insoluble problem. The main stream of the river was mapped by British, French and German explorers in the Egyptian service, by the year 1841, as far south as Gondokoro. John Petherick, a Cornish ivory-trader, was British consul at Khartoum in 1853.

The antiquities of Egypt were fully revealed to Europe by the expedition of Bonaparte in 1798 and the learned men who followed after. Among them may be mentioned the German linguist J. L. Burckhardt (1784–1817), of Göttingen and Cambridge, who went up the Nile to Assuan, visited Abyssinia, penetrated to Mecca in disguise (1815), and described the ruins of Palmyra and Baalbek. From the earliest times the Arab lands have exercised a strange fascination over some of the strongest English characters. First in the role of these English eccentrics is the name of Lady Hester Stanhope (1776–1839), who lost her employment when her uncle Pitt, for whom she kept house, died in 1806, and her lover when Sir John Moore fell at Corunna in 1809. She set out in the following year for the Levant, where she came to exercise a commanding influence over the Bedouin, always respectful to those whom Allah has afflicted. Growing crazier as she grew older, she yet retained an air of the best society and, royally if oddly, entertained other English travellers at her mountain fortress in the Lebanon. One of her visitors was that very superior person, A. W. Kinglake (1809–91), when he made the tour through Sinai and Syria commemorated in *Eothen*. Syrian, Persian and Arabian archaeology drew a succession of French, German and English travellers to the Levant, among them Sir A. H. Layard (1817–94) who excavated Nineveh in 1845. He was employed as a political adviser by Palmerston and later rose to be ambassador at Constantinople during the Russo-Turkish War. Sir H. C. Rawlinson (1810–95), an Indian Civilian, was sent as consul to Bagdad. A profound Persian scholar, he distinguished himself by deciphering the inscriptions of King Darius at Behistun. Another sort of traveller was W. C. Palgrave (1826–88), who went through Arabia in disguise on behalf of a Jesuit mission. Later, abandoning his creed, he undertook a political mission to Abyssinia in 1865. The coastal region of southern Arabia and Persia was visited by many political agents from India, notably Sir Lewis Pelly (1825–92), who led a mission from Bombay in 1860.

At the time of the occupation of Egypt the British authorities employed as a linguist Professor E. H. Palmer (1840–82) of Cambridge, a self-educated young man with a remarkable knowledge of oriental dialects. A precursor of the more celebrated T. E. Lawrence, he undertook to ingratiate the tribes of Sinai during the Egyptian War, but was killed by the Bedouin. Neither misanthropy nor political intrigue formed any part of the motive of Doctor Charles Doughty (1843–1926) who travelled alone through central Arabia in 1873–6 and wrote the strange rich odyssey, *Arabia Deserta,* to which all later travellers in that region are indebted. An unassuming Christian, he scorned disguise, moving freely and alone among fanatical Arabs, a poor man who went about doing good. He had a low opinion of Sir Richard Burton, who boasted of having made the pilgrimage to Mecca disguised as a Moslem.

Hardly less mysterious than the sources of the Nile was the course of the River Niger which was rumoured to flow past Timbuktu, but whether eastward or westward was not known. Perhaps it emerged on the Atlantic coast under the name of the Senegal or Gambia; perhaps in the Gulf of Guinea where there was a delta known as the Oil Rivers and an estuary known as the Congo. The investigation of this problem was undertaken by the African Association (1788) in which Sir Joseph Banks was a principal. This was the first of a series of efforts to open the way into the Niger basin in the joint interests of evangelism and commerce, which no one doubted to be ancillary to one another. The African Association (reorganised in 1830 as the Royal Geographical Society) despatched a number of expeditions to the Niger from north, south and west, most of them failures with loss of life. Their general effect was to confirm Europe in the view that West Africa was the White Man's Grave.

The most celebrated of these voyages, since the author's memoir of it is a masterpiece, was made by Mungo Park (1771–1806), a young Scottish surgeon who entered the service of the African Association in 1795. Setting out from the Gambia he crossed the Senegal River, made his way to Bamako on the Niger and returned (1797) after struggling alone and unarmed through almost unbelievable hardships. For seven or eight years he lived the quiet life of a country doctor at Peebles, where he won the friendship of Sir Walter Scott; then he was again sent to the Niger at the head of a large expedition financed by the Colonial Office. In November 1805 he sent back word to the Gambia that he was descending the Niger in a boat built by his men. There the story ends. Years later, reports filtered through from native traders that he and his few surviving comrades were drowned in a scuffle with Hausa tribesmen. Several succeeding expeditions also came to grief.

The first European to enter Timbuktu was Major A. G. Laing (1793–1826) who made his way there across the Sahara from Tripoli and was killed by the Touaregs on the return journey. A Frenchman, Réné Caillié, made a successful visit in the following year (1827) from the west and planted the seeds of French influence. The problem of the Niger, meanwhile, had been attacked by another British expedition from Tripoli. Two officers, Lieutenant H. Clapperton, R.N. (1788–1827), and Lieutenant D. Denham, 23rd Regiment (1786–1828), crossed the desert to Lake Chad which they were the first Europeans to visit (1823). Two of their English companions died, and their progress westward towards the Niger was obstructed by the powerful Fula kings who ruled the walled cities of Kano and Sokoto. Clapperton made a second attempt, after returning to Tripoli, and on this occasion approached the Niger from the Oil Coast. He crossed the river to die at Sokoto. His work was completed by his personal servant, Richard Lander (1804–34), a valet, had accompanied Clapperton on all his travels. Lander returned to England and persuaded government to finance a third expedition led by himself and his younger brother. They marched from the Oil Coast to the Niger, then paddled for two months downstream, emerging by the channel known as the Brass River (1830). The Oil Rivers were thus proved to be the outlet of the Niger. Richard Lander was killed in a fight with natives when on another visit to the delta.

The savannah country between the Niger and Lake Chad was made known in general outline by the travels (1852–6) of Dr Heinrich Barth of Hamburg, who was despatched from the north by the British government.

During the 'fifties the centre of interest shifted back from the Niger to the Nile, and at this point it will be proper to introduce the swashbuckling figure of Sir Richard Burton (1821–90), the translator of the *Arabian Nights*. He was bred at Oxford and, if he is to be given a professional label, we must call him a philologist. After serving in the Bombay Army he began a wandering life in Moslem India, winning fame in 1853 by his pilgrimage to Mecca which he described in a forceful literary style. Next he attempted to penetrate Somaliland with J. H. Speke (1827–64) a fellow-soldier from India; then served a campaign in the Crimea. In 1857 Burton was despatched by the Royal Geographical Society to corroborate the tale told by Dr Ludwig Krapf, the missionary, of snowy mountains and inland seas in the heart of

Africa. He set out with Speke from Zanzibar. But Burton was a sharp-tongued fellow, ill to reckon with, and Speke parted from him on the shores of Lake Tanganyika, the first of the Great African Lakes to be discovered. Speke found the southern shore of Lake Victoria, and Burton disbelieved his story. Speke came home first and claimed the credit of the voyage with the result that he was sent by the Society on a further trip to find the source of the Nile. With a new companion, J. A. Grant (1827–92), he saw the main stream of the river issue from Lake Victoria (28 July 1862), but his travels added little to precise geographical knowledge since he was no surveyor. Speke and Grant followed the stream down until they met another English traveller coming up the river to meet them. This was Sir Samuel Baker, a rich adventurer and sportsman who had come south from Egypt with his wife and a well-equipped party. Speke first among Europeans saw the source of the Nile; Baker explored and surveyed the region on information supplied by Speke. Later as Governor of the Equatorial Province (1869–73) Baker served the Khedive of Egypt in suppressing the slave trade. Speke was killed in a shooting accident soon after his return to England.

The discomfited Burton transferred his efforts elsewhere. He held consular appointments at Fernando Po, Damascus, Santos, and Trieste which enabled him to travel adventurously and to write vigorously about Arabia, West Africa and Brazil.

When the message was telegraphed from Khartoum in 1863 that the source of the Nile had at last been found ('The Nile is settled'), it produced a new enthusiasm for the opening of Central Africa. This wonderland of lakes and mountains, which Burton, Speke and Baker had revealed, must be explored, civilised and cleansed from the horrors of the slave trade. The stage was set for the entrance of the hero who appeared in the person of David Livingstone, then at the height of his fame.

Through Livingstone's memoirs the public became acquainted with the features of African travel. They could picture the clear sunshine beating on the red dusty plateau that makes up ninetenths of the continent; the files of negro porters, led by standard-bearers and drum-mers, bearing bundles on their heads through the tall grass in which grew like living things the domed or pinnacled ant-heaps; they could smell the hot spicy scents of the crowded markets where Livingstone's heart overflowed with kindness towards the smiling, hard-bargaining, cheerful Africans. In parklike glades the herds of game glanced up and vanished into the scrub as though scorning the slow-footed humans; the lions roared after their prey by night; the snow-white cranes and egrets and kingfishers flew over shining lakes and rivers towards glimpses of inaccessible mountains. And all was afflicted by the ten plagues of Pharaoh, with tsetse-fly, fever, hailstorms, swarms ol locusts, and last of all with slaughter and death.

David Livingstone (1813–73) was working in a cotton-mill at Blantyre at the age of ten. He educated himself and was accepted for service abroad, in 1838, by the London Missionary Society. After awaiting an appointment for two years, which he spent in studying medicine at Glasgow, he was selected to serve with Robert Moffatt in South Africa. On the voyage to the Cape he persuaded the ship's captain to instruct him in navigation and thereafter 'took his daily observations as regularly as he said his prayers'. In 1841 he went up to Kuruman in Bechuanaland to join Moffatt, whose daughter he soon married.

Though eclipsed by his greater son-in-law, Robert Moffatt (1795–1883) makes no small figure in the sphere of missionary enterprise. He opened the 'Missionaries' Road' along the eastern fringe of the Kalahari Desert, settled among the Bechuana (1825), and even came eventually to exercise some influence over Moselikatze, the first King of the Matabele (about 1859). While Moffatt devoted his life to preaching and converting, Livingstone was rather a pioneer of missions, hailing with delight the decision taken by the Society, 'that we go forward to the dark interior'.

After several excursions westward across the Kalahari and northwards towards the Zambezi, in one of which he was mauled by a lion, he sent his wife and children to England and plunged into the unknown. In his absence his house and papers were ravaged by Boer filibusters who already knew him as a protector of natives against exploitation, and hated him.

The first of Livingstone's three great expeditions was his crossing and recrossing of Africa (1853–6) from the middle Zambezi to Loanda on the West Coast, and back to Quilimane on the East. In November 1855 he discovered the Victoria Falls. This series of marches, without white companions and on foot, among primitive tribes who were mightly impressed by his dauntless simplicity was perhaps his greatest and most typical exploit. Thereafter men from his favourite Makololo tribe, his 'faithfuls', followed him to the end of his life. On this expedition, too, he first came upon the beastly evidences of Arab slavers, and was obliged to admit that Portuguese traders backed their efforts. He then devoted his life to combating the slave trade by moral influence, his method being to let light into Darkest Africa so that Christian civilisation could prove its worth.

In 1856 Livingstone returned to England to find that the publication of his *Missionary Travels and Researches* made him famous. The precision of his observations won him recognition from the Royal Society, the Royal Geographical Society and the universities; and his appeal in the Senate House at Cambridge (4 December 1857) led to the foundation of the Universities' Mission to Central Africa. 'I beg to direct your attention to Africa', he said. 'I know that in a few years I shall be cut off in that country, which is now open; do not let it be shut again. I go back to Africa to try to make an open path for commerce and Christianity; do you carry out the work which I have begun. I leave it with you.' He resigned from the London Missionary Society (though not through any change of principle) in order to accept a post as consul at Quilimane which would enable him to explore the country north of the Zambezi, where he was to establish the Universities' Mission, with a government grant of £5000.

His second great expedition began when he left Quilimane (1858) in an ocean-going steam-launch at the head of a party including Dr John Kirk. This was not so happy an experience for Livingstone as his earlier travels. He was out of his element when in command of white men. Nor did the attempt to explore by river-steamer prove successful since the Zambezi, like most Africa rivers, is blocked by cataracts. Yet the explorers entered the Shiré country (where now the town of Blantyre is named after Livingstone's birthplace), and discovered Lake Nyasa. The country was ravaged by slave-raiders with whom it was difficult to avoid fighting when they obstructed progress. Two misfortunes fell in 1862, when Bishop C. F. Mackenzie, who had come out to start the Universities' Mission, died of fever, and when Livingstone's wife also died while visiting him. In 1863 the expedition was withdrawn for lack of funds.

Though Livingstone was deeply grieved, he abated nothing of his courage. Since he could find no market for his steam-launch he characteristically sailed it across the Indian Ocean to sell it in Bombay before returning to London (1864), where he was lionised again. Lord Palmerston and the best Whig society made much of him. Though Livingstone was now past fifty and weakened by dysentery after his Zambezi voyage, he was persuaded by Sir R. Murchison, the President of the Royal Geographical Society, to return once more to Africa. The work of Speke and Baker must be completed. Had they indeed found the ultimate source of the Nile or was there another tributary stream beyond Lake Tanganyika? This was Burton's view, and Livingstone, who rather favoured it, sought confirmation in traditions preserved by Herodotus. Livingstone's third and longest expedition was geographical;

he was to find and explore the central watershed of Africa between Lakes Tanganyika and Nyasa. For all his popularity the money provided was meagre, and he went to Bombay to collect the sale-price of his steamboat. There he won the enthusiastic support of the Governor, Sir Bartle Frere, who gave him a letter to the Sultan of Zanzibar and a detachment of Indian sepoys. Frere also arranged for Livingstone's old comrade, Dr John Kirk, to be appointed to the consulate at Zanzibar.

In 1866 Livingstone was mustering his resources at Zanzibar in an atmosphere that he heartily disliked. The taint of the slave market corrupted slaves and slave-owners alike. His train of porters from this depraved society proved idle and mutinous from the start. Even Livingstone's example failed to charm them into honourable courses. The *banians* who provided his stores and the Arab chiefs who lorded it over the coastal region, though obliged to respect his authority as a British consul approved by the Sultan, yet knew that his life-work was to destroy the trade in 'black ivory' by which they lived. They thwarted him politely and frustrated all Kirk's endeavours to send replenishments to the advanced base which, on Speke's advice, he proposed to form at Ujiji, beside Lake Tanganyika. Once away from Zanzibar he was more solitary in Africa than ever before. His porters mutinied, deserted, pilfered; the sepoys proved useless for African travel; only his 'faithfuls' were any comfort to him. Soon an ominous recurrence of ill-health began to be noted in his journal. His mighty frame was wearing out, and the loss of his medicine-chest, stolen by a deserter, was a sore blow. He roved through Central Africa, seeking his river, for more than seven years (1866–73) but was seen only once again by any white man.

No sooner had he vanished up-country than a tribal war broke out behind him cutting off all communication with the coast. Later the cholera came, decimating Zanzibar and depopulating the countryside. In 1866 one parcel of despatches came through, and then a rumour that he was dead. Next year a relief expedition went up Lake Nyasa, found evidence that he was alive, but failed to make contact. After a long pause another letter reached the coast in 1868; then nothing.

The world wondered, while the old man marched and countermarched about Lake Tanganyika in failing health. In 1868 he found Lake Bangweulu; in 1869 he came to Ujiji to find that the stores sent by Kirk had been looted. For a long time he was obliged to live on the charity of Arab chiefs whom he found 'very gentlemanly slavers'. They protected him, thwarted him, and made no secret of their real business. At last in March 1871 he discovered a broad clear river, the Lualaba, flowing north and made sure it must be the headwaters of the Nile, but by no means could he obtain a boat to launch on it. On 13 October 1871 he fell back to Ujiji shockingly ill, with neither food nor drugs nor trade goods and with a mere handful of followers; and there five days later the relief expedition of H. M. Stanley found him.

Livingstone was relieved by Stanley, not lost and found; for Stanley encountered him just where he was supposed to be. Refreshed by Stanley's company and re-equipped by his bounty, Livingstone resumed his quest without any thought of withdrawing before his task was accomplished. After the two parted, in March 1872, Livingstone explored the region between the Lakes for a whole year more, while disease and weakness slowly mastered him. He made no more great discoveries but would not falter, though his daily marches shortened. When he could no longer march he rode a donkey, and when he could no longer ride he was borne in a litter, but still pressed on. If he could he would have died marching and, since he could not, he died praying. On 1 May 1873 his 'faithfuls' found him dead, kneeling at his bedside. Not the least heroic episode in his saga is the decision of his 'boys', Susi and Chuma, to hold the expedition together. They marched back as they had come, through 800 miles of wilderness, from Lake Bangweulu to Zanzibar, carrying their master's body and the record of his work. On the way they met another relieving expedition which had come too late. Its leader, Lieutenant V. L. Cameron, went on to finish Livingstone's task. The old man had been at fault; his Lualaba River was the Congo not the Nile.

Meanwhile Stanley had scooped the greatest newspaper sensation of the decade, and exploited it in lecture-tours and in a book: *How I Found Livingstone*.

In the final opening of Africa, H. M. Stanley (1841–1904) played no small part. His own story was hardly less remarkable than the epic life of Livingstone, though by his own account it rather resembled a serial story in a magazine for boys. He ran away to sea from a Welsh workhouse after thrashing the Mr Squeers who had ill-treated him there. Later when befriended by an American named Stanley, the boy adopted his benefactor's name and nationality. In the Civil War he managed the surprising feat of fighting on both sides, first in the Confederate Army and then in the Federal Navy. After skirmishing with Red Indians in the West, and coming through a scrape with brigands in Asia Minor, he turned up at the Abyssinian War as special reporter for the New York *Herald*. By bribing the telegraph clerk he got his first 'scoop', an exclusive account of the fall of Magdala, which made him ripe for higher flights of journalism. In October 1869, his editor, Gordon Bennett, summoned Stanley to Paris to receive several assignments; he was to go to Persia and India for this and that, to attend the opening of the Suez Canal and, when he got around to it, he was to find Dr Livingstone, not because the Doctor needed help but because he made headline news. Fifteen months passed before Stanley came to Zanzibar and there he was so blatant in his gossip-columnist's method, so secretive about his real intention, so careless of the company he kept, that he antagonised John Kirk and all Livingstone's friends. Without their help he proved himself a master of the art of tropical travel, perhaps because he had unlimited funds; and marched up the country beneath the Stars and Stripes, in record time, not achieved without a liberal use of whip and gun. Forcing his way through opposition he arrived, as has been already told, at Ujiji.

As I come nearer [so runs his record] I see the white face of an old man. . . . He has a cap with a gold band round it; his dress is a short jacket of red blanket cloth, and his pants—well, I didn't observe; I am shaking hands with him. We raise our hats and I say, 'Dr. Livingstone, I presume?' And he says 'Yes'.

The banality of that famous utterance, bringing world-wide movements and opposed generations into a single focus, like a snapshot of a historical crisis, was at once fixed as one of the undying myths of the Anglo-Saxon race. The old age and the new met and recognised one another. There was the simple old Scottish saint, as plain and resolute as one of his own covenanting ancestors, one of the most famous men alive but intent only on his self-allotted duty; and there was the Anglo-American publicity-hunter, nigger-driving through Africa with all the blare and bounce of the yellow press. Yet Livingstone drew new life from the adventurous youngster who brought him relief, friendship, conversation, news; and Stanley, in spite of his coarser fibre, knew that to serve Livingstone and win his affection was the supreme experience of his career. His flashy journalism is tinged with reverence when he speaks of the Doctor: 'In him there is no guile and what is apparent on the surface is the thing that is in him. His gentleness never forsakes him; his hopefulness never deserts him. Religion has tamed him and made him a Christian gentleman'. With this tale Stanley returned to England where he was genuinely shocked to learn that many people thought him vulgar and pretentious, while some doubted the truth of his story. He weakened his case by belittling Livingstone's other friends, especially John Kirk, in order to heighten the effect of his own exploit. The Queen was one of the first to make allowances and to give him credit.

In 1873 Stanley was off again to Ashanti with Wolseley's expedition.

In 1874 he was persuaded by Burnham of the *Telegraph* and Bennett
of the New York *Herald* to undertake the exploration of the Congo.
This was (1874–7) perhaps the most fruitful of all African expeditions.
After tracing the whole course of the river he marched through the
rain-forest to the Lakes, surveyed Lake Victoria, discovered Lake
Edward and revealed to the world the kingdom of Uganda, the most
advanced of African polities. The first to grasp the meaning of his
discoveries was King Leopold of Belgium who sent to meet him as he
returned, with consequences that will be considered in the next chap-
ter.[1] After four years of strenuous pioneering in the Congo State
(1879–83) he made his last expedition to Africa in search of Emin
Pasha and then withdrew from active travel though not from lecture-
tours. As he grew older he became more favourable to British policy,
resumed his British nationality, accepted a knighthood, stood for
Parliament as a Liberal-unionist and married into one of the best
families. He died in 1904 at the age of sixty-three.

By that time Africa was mapped, partitioned and subjugated. A
stream of missionaries and explorers, inspired by Livingstone's example,
had followed the trail he blazed. The slave trade had been stopped
or driven out of sight; and after it vanished tribal wars, cannibalism,
human sacrifice. In the new Africa of the twentieth century the long
laborious fight against ignorance, poverty and disease was beginning.

NOTES

Samuel Baker, *Albert N'Yanza, Great Basin of the Nile, and Explorations
of the Nile,* London, 1866.
David Livingstone, *Livingstone's African Journal, 1853–1856* (I. Schapera,
ed.), Berkeley, 1963.
Alan Moorehead, *The White Nile,* New York, 1961; *The Blue Nile,* New
York, 1962.
Mungo Park, *The Life and Travels of Mungo Park,* London, 1815.
George Seaver, *David Livingstone,* London, 1957.
Henry M. Stanley, *How I Found Livingstone,* New York, 1872; *Through the
the Dark Continent,* 2 Vol., New York, 1878.

[1] Not reprinted here, however; the interested reader is referred to the original
book.

HOW MEN FIND OIL *

E. L. De Golyer

A recent book entitled The Greatest Gamblers: The Epic of American Oil Exploration *is dedicated "To all the unsuccessful explorers who have drilled America's 300,000 dry holes and whose failures have guided others to the discovery of an abundance of oil." But along with the account of those explorers who failed to become discoverers, it has much to say about the fortunate ones whose gushers kept gushing. The immediate rewards for the successful discoveries—for individuals, corporations, and for countries—have been higher than for most previous exploring because of the steadily increasing world demand for petroleum.*

This quest for riches beneath the surface has had much in common with the prospecting for gold in the previous century, resulting in huge findings in California, Australia, South Africa, and British Columbia. Thousands had hunches that there was "gold in them thar' hills," but as in the search for petroleum, the lucky ones were only a small minority.

The great age of oil discovery has coincided with the twentieth century. There had been a moderate growth of the oil industry ever since the beginning at Titusville, Pennsylvania, in 1859. Further deposits were discovered in adjacent states, but the production was on a relatively modest scale, most of the crude oil being converted into kerosene, which supplanted whale oil for illumination.

The twentieth century was not quite two weeks old when the first great oil strike was made, on January 13, 1901, at "Spindletop" in eastern Texas, not far from the Louisiana border. Then, in quick succession, one state after another shot into first place in oil production as a result of new discovery, the first leader being California, where oil was found even within the limits of Los Angeles. Kansas and Oklahoma came prominently into the picture, but Texas finally secured first place. In the early years of the century the rapid development of the automobile shifted the demand from kerosene to gasoline, and tractors and then airplanes also played their part. Before long there was a heavy additional call for fuel oil for ships, factories, and general heating. Meanwhile

* E. L. De Golyer, "How Men Find Oil," Fortune, August 1949, XLVI, pp. 97–104. By permission of Fortune.

natural gas, found in great quantities along with the oil, added to the value of the new findings.

Although the United States had a long head start in oil discovery and production, the mounting demand led to searches elsewhere, Adjacent Mexico gained temporary prominence, but Venezuela had more lasting success when huge oil deposits were discovered under the shallow waters of Lake Maracaibo.

At the same time, exploration was revealing another great oil region in the Middle East. An energetic Australian, D'Arcy, already lucky in gold mining, got a concession from Persia (now Iran) for oil and other mineral deposits, but it was only after several years of frustrating delays that oil was finally discovered; the Anglo-Persian Oil Company was formed in time to provide the British Navy with fuel oil. That was just the beginning for the Middle East. Oil was soon discovered around Mosul in the present Iraq, and then in even greater quantities in the barren, sandy regions of the Persian Gulf and Southern Arabia. Little sheikhdoms like Kuwait and Bahrein suddenly grew fabulously rich from their royalty shares of the output. Some of the initial exploration and discovery here and elsewhere was the work of individual wildcatters, as the hardy gamblers searching in new regions were called, but other exploration and most of the development was in the hands of the big American or British oil companies, whose deep pockets could absorb the heavy costs and risks. It is said that Standard Oil of New Jersey (Esso) spent $48 million in preliminary exploration in Venezuela before the first barrel of crude oil was pumped.

The quest has continued in many parts of the world—every country is keenly aware of the advantage of an oil supply either for its own use or for export. Large oil deposits have been found in widely scattered places, all the way from Alberta in Canada to the Sahara Desert—not only in Algeria but also in adjacent Libya, which was transformed overnight from dire poverty to high prosperity. Outside of Rumania and southern Russia, little oil has been discovered in Europe, but the recent finding of oil deposits under the waters of the North Sea has brought forth rival claims from adjacent countries, hoping for a supply close to home.

The following article was written by Everette L. De Golyer, one of the most successful of all expert consultants on the locating of oil.

"How did you discover the Panuco field?" I teased Professor Cummins one sultry summer day as we sat in his Tampico office. The patriarch stroked his long white beard and looked thoughtful. That was forty years ago. Both of us were geologists and knew that the field lay in the broad alluvial plain of the Panuco River in northeastern Mexico, miles from the nearest significant rock outcrop. There hadn't been a single damned reason, that I could see, to think that it was a good location. The professor looked up at the ceiling and shook his head. Then he looked at me, seriously, as though he were trying to determine whether or not I could be worthy of a great secret:

"Been asked that question many times. Never made any answer— too technical." His best eye gleamed. "Goin' to tell you, though—you c'n understand." A long pause. With a triumphant snap of the end of his beard, he leaned forward and whispered, "Little bird told me."

Panuco developed into a great oil field and I thought that the professor was pretty lucky. Well, he was. It takes luck to discover oil. Prospecting is like gin rummy. Luck enough will win but not skill alone. Best of all are luck and skill in proper proportion, but don't ask what the proportion should be. In case of doubt, weight mine with luck.

Cummins was an old circuit rider. In the early eighties he abandoned the saddlebags for geology but still preached occasionally. The professor was considered one of the "characters" in the saga of oil-field geology in North America. But in making a study of the history of oil prospecting years later, I came to a more correct appreciation of the old professor's professional achievement.

At the age of sixty-nine, after many years of geological work and some of oil-field management in Texas, he crossed the Rio Grande into Mexico. For months he worked slowly southward, past the great anticlinal arch of the Sierra de San Carlos and Sierra de Tamaulipas, to the Panuco River. A projection of the axis of this arch would pass near the town of Panuco and the meanders of the river rather suggest broad anticlinal structure. (An anticline is an upfold or dome in the rocks.) True there was an oil seepage a few kilometers away near Tampalache, but the professor did not crowd it. He took leases for his employer, the East Coast Oil Co., and completed the discovery well in September, 1910.

The extension of mountain folding, which Professor Cummins appears to have recognized, developed over the years into a great district of many pools and has produced a total of more than 800 million barrels of oil. This was a beautiful piece of constructive geological reasoning.

Oil fields have been found by accident. They have been found for good reason, for bad reason, and for no reason at all. Spiritualists and divining-rod men, dowsers if we must be exact, have contributed to the prospecting effort. They still do, for that matter, as witness the skillful operator who wiggle-sticked the discovery of the West Edmond pool in Oklahoma. Men have drawn odd lines on maps connecting known oil fields as far apart as Pennslyvania and California, Alberta and Louisiana,

and have worked themselves into a frenzy of excitement over the pre-
sumed attractiveness of the point where the lines intersected.

You might do any of these things, or even find some new and equally
weird scheme of your own for locating a well, and be successful. It is a
costly experiement, however, and probably would fail. In 1948, 6,182
wildcat wells were drilled in the U.S. They cost about a billion dollars,
and seven out of eight were dry.

Most of the world's early production was found by men who knew
no more of origin or occurrence of oil than they did of the inner work-
ings of a slot machine. They drilled. They pulled the lever and hoped
for the jackpot. We still don't know much about origin. It is commonly
accepted that oil is distilled by earth heat and pressure from organic
matter, chiefly plant, buried in the sediments of ancient seas—an origin
resembling in its initial stages that of coal. But we really don't need to
know about origin. A hunter will fare better knowing the habits of
quail than knowing the period of incubation of their eggs or even that
they hatch from eggs.

We had better learn something about occurrence, however, if we
want to understand modern prospecting. That's habit. Unlike coal,
which stays where it is formed, oil is moved around by circulating
waters. And in the search for oil, we are concerned only with the places
where it has been collected into pools.

What is an oil pool like? Oil and gas bubbling upward through
water can be trapped into bubbles of larger volume by holding one's
cupped hand immersed and palm downward over the stream of bubbles.
An oil and gas pool in the earth is essentially a great bubble floating on
a sea of salt water, its shape and extent modified by the form, thickness,
and extent of the porous rock in which it is contained. In our experiment
the cupped hand has served two functions essential to accumulation:
(1) it has blocked oil and gas from traveling farther, the cap rock function; (2) by its cupped shape a trap was formed into which oil and gas
bubbles carried by circulating waters could be accumulated into a pool.

A Seepage Is a Good Sign

The trap's the thing. Almost the sole business of the modern oil
prospector is a search for underground traps. The drill alone can determine whether the trap contains commercial oil and gas. Even a most
perfect trap in a most prolific region may be dry. Such a trap within
sight of the mammoth East Texas oil field has been drilled repeatedly
without success. Even with the benefit of all the scientific knowledge

available, oil prospecting, no matter how attractive the prospect may be, is still a matter of chance. The drill is the final arbiter.

The Drake well, which was drilled at Oil Creek, Pennsylvania, in 1859, is the well from which we commonly reckon the beginning of the industry. It was drilled near an oil seepage by men who could have known no more of the occurrence of oil than that it occasionally bubbled up through springs, sometimes saturated the outcrop of porous rocks, often appeared in brine wells, and, vaguely, that it was associated with natural gas. They followed instinct as old as man's mining experience and dug a hole in search of a more abundant supply of the mineral found at the surface.

The industry during its first half century was pretty small potatoes. We now produce in a single year almost as much oil as was produced in the entire period. Prospecting was without technical guidance. The oil seepage continued to be the cynosure, particularly for new regions. As experience grew, vague theories, mostly worthless, began to develop.

The Drake well was drilled in the valley of a meandering stream and for a short while it was held that oil could be found only in valleys. This theory was blown sky-high when some daring wildcatter found oil in the hills.

Numerology May Work

As fields were extended by stepping out from existing wells, it became apparent that their major axes generally followed the same direction or strike. This gave rise to the "belt line" theory, which was, essentially, that land along this strike in either direction from proved wells was the preferred area in which to prospect. When valid, this strike represented either the main structural strike of the region or the region's stratigraphic grain—the direction of old shorelines on which sands had been deposited. The theory fell into disrepute because of the failures arising out of rigid adherence to it. It became ludicrous when a strike determined by trial and error for a specific region—N.22½° E. was the favorite for Pennsylvania—was transferred boldly over hundreds of miles to an entirely different part of the country.

The early prospectors were resourceful, however, and used to cobble their errors by halving the bearing. If N.22½° E. would not work in early Oklahoma–Kansas prospecting, try N.11° E. If this did not work, try N.5° or 6° E., which came pretty near to fact. Such is the magic of numerical mumbo jumbo.

The old terms "belt" and "belt line" have long been forgotten. The technique, however, was a crude geological method developed by the industry. In lieu of other and better methods it still has value and survives under the names of "trend" and "trend lines." I have long held that if geology had not existed already as a science, necessity would have forced the industry to create and develop it. The history of the old "belt line" theory supports my belief.

Within a few months after the completion of the Drake well, geologists began to speculate on the nature of oil occurrence. Among the earliest proposed was the anticlinal theory. The dome of an anticline is one of the commonest forms of trap occurring in nature—the equivalent again of the cupped hand of our experiment. The theory had hard going in early days. It was restricted to a single form of trap and it had the bad luck to be proposed while the chief oil development was still in the Appalachian region, one in which oil occurs chiefly in stratigraphic traps and anticlinal occurrence is uncommon. There is little enough to be done from the surface in searching for stratigraphic traps. Wells were about the only method of prospecting for this type of occurrence and they were still shallow and fairly cheap.

When the industry was faced with the sharp upturn in demand for its products that came as the motor age really got under way about 1910, it found itself with a job bigger than the gray-haired practical men could handle. Prospecting become a part of the day-by-day business of the industry to an extent not true for any other mineral industry.

Science Gets on the Payroll

It was about the turn of the century that geologists came into the oil industry. And from 1910 to 1915 they pretty well took over direction of its prospecting. It was their business to search for traps. They amended the anticlinal theory until at last they found the least common denominator—the trap.

Obviously there are a great variety of geological conditions that may form traps. There are many types of traps, but their primary classification is that of structural traps and stratigraphic traps. This classification tells us little or nothing about origin. Its value is wholly practical, for we have much greater ability to prospect for structural than for stratigraphic-type traps. Anticlines, fault blocks, salt domes, faulting and fissuring, and in rare instances even the intrusion of volcanic rocks—these are called the structural traps.

Stratigraphic traps are zones of porous rock turned into reservoirs by something that limits the porosity and blocks the outflow of oil. Blocking may occur in a great number of ways. Frequently—as in the huge East Texas field—the porous zone simply tapers off between layers of nonporous rock. But some stratigraphic traps are quite complex. In the Ras Gharib field of Egypt, a sequence of deposition, tilting, erosion, faulting, and deposition again, was required to form an effective trap.

In early prospecting, the geologist studied and mapped the rocks either by determining with clinometer the degree and direction of dip of the individual outcrop or by traversing and determining the elevation of an individual recognizable bed of rock. He assumed parallelism between outcropping and deeply buried beds. This was a fair assumption, but better methods for discovering traps were slowly evolved.

Beaumont's Great Gusher

The Gulf Coast was brought into production and great wealth by Captain Anthony F. Lucas. On a bright January morning in 1901 he and his crew were busy about the derrick in his second attempt to find oil at Spindletop. They kept at it although Captain Lucas had been advised against the venture by top-drawer experts of Standard Oil and of the U.S. Geological Survey. Suddenly the drill stem started to come slowly out of the hole. The tool dresser skinned down from the top of the derrick in alarm. The drill stem shot through the crown block to a height of 500 feet, carrying with it the heavy tackle of the rig. Poised for an instant, it swayed like a reed in the breeze, then came crashing to the ground. It was followed immediately by the remaining drill stem, while the men scurried to safety. Oil and gas burst out of the hole with a terrific roar and a glistening black geyser gushed through the derrick and a good 200 feet into the air. Away across the prairie from this black demon, farmer Ingalls lashed his horse to carry the news to Beaumont, a sleepy little lumber town on the Neches River. The well flowed wild for ten days at the rate of 50,000 to 100,000 barrels daily. It was the biggest well the U.S. had ever seen and it was almost a thousand miles from the nearest important oil field. It was emphatic proof that oil might be found anywhere, and with the completion of the discovery well the modern oil industry was born.

Spindletop production came from the cap and overlying sands of a salt dome. Salt domes are formed by the forcing upward of a great boss or plug of rock salt in plastic flow from deep in the earth. Only the upper part of any of the Gulf coastal salt plugs has been explored. The salt masses are generally flat-topped, circular to elliptical in plane section, and they vary from less than a mile to several miles in their major axes. They stand up from unknown depths as gigantic columns or as great truncated cones. A cap of porous limestone, gypsum, and anhydrite usually covers the blunt top of the salt and sometimes extends thimble-like down its sides. The intrusion of one of these plugs tilts the beds pierced by it so that they dip away in all directions. Traps that may contain oil are commonly found in the sediments arched over the plug, in the lime-stone-anhydrite cap, or in the funnellike structure of the pierced beds. Spindletop was such a dome.

Salt Without Oil

The only surface expression of the salt domes known or suspected in the time of Captain Lucas was a low topographic mound, sometimes with gas or oil seepages or springs of sour water. Two or three of the mounds reach elevations of one hundred to three hundred feet but most of them rise over an area of a few hundred acres, only ten to twenty feet above the flat plain. Such slight expression would be almost impossible to recognize except by careful leveling in any land less flat than the Gulf Coast littoral.

Within three to five years after the Spindletop completion all such topographic mounds or sizable seepages of known oil and gas had been drilled. A number of important oil fields were found but most of the tests failed. In all, as a result of this campaign of exploration, some thirty-five to forty salt domes had been discovered.

There followed a humdrum twenty years of the most discouraging type of prospecting. By following the most intangible clues or even by random drilling, approximately six new domes were found. Some seven hundred wildcat wells were drilled at a cost of more than $20 million to achieve this result.

At this point geophysics came to the rescue of the industry and of geology with the introduction into the Gulf Coast region of the torsion balance. This was in late 1922 and, although I was partly responsible for its introduction, I may as well admit that I have never understood the functioning of that delicate instrument well enough to explain it clearly. It is an adaptation to field use by the Hungarian physicist, Baron Roland Eötvös, of the Coulomb torsion balance, which has been used in physical laboratories since the eighteenth century for investigating and demonstrating the laws of gravitational attraction. The field instrument was used to search for anomalies in the earth's gravity field. Since such anomalies were usually the result of unequal distribution of masses of rock of different specific gravities, they were effectively geological anomalies as well, and might indicate the existence of traps. (The gravimeter, which performs a similar function, was introduced in 1931 and by 1933 had rendered the torsion balance practically obsolete.)

In the spring of 1924 the first refraction seismograph to work in the U.S. appeared on the Gulf Coast. In this method a series of longitudinal, compressional, elastic waves—let's settle for sound waves—is generated by the explosion of dynamite near the earth's surface, and the time of their travel to an instrument a known distance away (usually several miles) is recorded with a precision up to one one-thousandth of a second. Sound waves travel at different velocities through different types of rock. For the Gulf Coast the velocity through clays, shales, and sands is normally around 6,000 feet a second. Through the dense rock salt of the domes it is 15,000 to 16,000 feet a second—nearly fifteen times the velocity of sound in air. If a salt plug comes to within 5,000 to 6,000 feet of the surface, its presence is indicated by the arrival of sound waves refracted through the salt in a shorter time than if no such high-velocity rock had been encountered. This "lead" in time of arrival was believed to indicate a salt dome if it amounted to as much as three-tenths of a second.

Dry Runs in the Bayous

This method could cover territory much more rapidly and its findings were more diagnostic than those of the torsion balance. With the early success of this method, a wild campaign of surveys swept the coast through Louisiana and Texas. One of the most successful of these surveys was that of some two million acres of swamps and water bottoms in southern Louisiana for the Louisiana Land & Exploration Co. This group of properties had been put together by Colonel Ed Simms, a famous wildcatter from Spindletop days.

"Are you sure, son, that there's a salt dome out there?" he demanded of me one morning as we stood at Cypremort Point on the shore of Vermilion Bay. We were peering across miles of open water at the dim outline of a derrick shimmering through a haze that the early Louisiana sun had not yet burned away. I waived the benevolent "son" but was still old enough to keep open a road for retreat. Oil geology is not one of the exact sciences. "Think so," I replied. "Ef that's so," declared the Colonel, "time for me to get out of the oil business. Don't make sense." The dome was there all right—and it's still a prospect. There isn't enough money in the Bank of England to prove that a salt dome is dry.

The campaign of refraction surveys covered the entire Gulf Coast from Corpus Christi to east of the Mississippi, much of it five and six times for different companies. It lasted about six years, cost some $25 million for geophysics alone, and resulted in doubling the number of domes known on the coast. Each new salt dome discovered, including those that produced no oil, had cost an average of over $600,000.

By about 1930 the value of the refraction technique for the Gulf Coast area, the only region in the U.S. where it was known to be useful, had been exhausted. There was practically no territory susceptible to examination that had not been surveyed. Within a matter of months a new method based on sound reflection was reduced to practice and became the dominant prospecting technique. It remains so to this day. It also is a seismic method but of much more widespread usefulness than the refraction method.

With the reflection or echo method, sound waves are generated by the explosion of dynamite at or near the surface. Their travel time to and from various deeply buried reflecting formations is recorded and the data obtained is used to determine the depth to point of reflection, with an error of one-half per cent or less. By correlation of depths so determined at many points, the geologic structure of the area surveyed can be mapped. The cost of seismic work, almost entirely by the reflection method, in the U.S. alone has totaled upwards of $600 million since the early thirties, and current expenditure is at an annual rate in excess of $50 million.

Hints for the Oil Prospector

What you do to find oil is somewhat like selecting the clubs to play different shots at golf. Let's suppose that you are an experienced prospector going into an almost unknown region. As a preliminary you will gather all possible information regarding its geology and oil indications. If available information is inadequate as a basis to plan your campaign of exploration, and it probably will be inadequate, you will make a reconnaissance of the area. I suspect you will search for oil seepages and, that chimera of oil geologists, so-called source beds—beds that look as though oil might have originated in them. If you had found an oil seepage in olden days you would have drilled near it without further ado. With modern techniques of examination available, however, you will regard this as involving unnecessary risks. Reassured as to the pertoliferous nature of the area, you will next map its surface geology. If this does not adequately reveal the stucture, you may supplement it by pit digging or core drilling. If favorable structure is found you are likely to drill a wildcat well.

In many areas, however, none of these methods apply, or even if they do and you want to be most exact, your last recourse is the geophysical methods. If a large area is involved you will probably survey it with an airborne magnetometer. Results are not likely to be diagnostic but you will obtain suggestions as to structural trends, perhaps as to stratigraphic grain, and guidance in spotting areas for more detailed exploration. You may then map the entire area, or such of its parts as appear attractive, with the gravimeter. Again, results may be so positive as to suggest drilling, but you are still cautious and check the exciting areas with the reflection-seismic method. Except for the new and still controversial geochemical methods (essentially the search for micro-seepages in soils, soil gases, or surface water), you will have exhausted your available techniques and will drill or abandon the area.

Maybe You're Sitting on Oil—Maybe

What about you, as a landowner? You may own a twenty-five-foot-front California chicken ranch or a King Ranch in Texas and be minded to try to find whether or not it is likely to be underlain by oil. If you insist, the methods you may use have been sketched. I advise you not to try it. There are something like eight to ten thousand vigorous and active young men who spend most of their waking hours and tremendous sums of money in scouring every corner of these United States in a search for oil. If your property includes or is part of an attractive prospect, you have heard or will hear from them or their companies. You can then decide whether to lease your land or hold it, pending completion of the exploratory well. If you decide not to accept this gratuitous advice, get together all of your money, all of your wife's money, and all you can borrow and go to it. But geophysical work alone has cost more than $105,000 a well for the several hundred exploratory wells drilled during the last five years in southern Louisiana. The leasing of a block and drilling of the wildcat well bring the total cost of a single prospect to more than three times that figure. You don't want to take that much risk on your land, do you? Especially when you can get an eighth of the production, bonuses and rentals by letting the oil companies take the chance. They make a business of it.

NOTES

Leonard M. Fanning, *The Rise of American Oil,* New York, 1936; *American Oil Interests Abroad,* New York, 1947.

Ruth S. Knowles, *The Greatest Gamblers: The Epic of American Oil Exploration,* New York, 1959.

Stephen H. Longrigg, *Oil in the Middle East: Its Discovery and Development* 2d ed., London, 1961.

Frederick A. Talbot, *The Oil Conquest of the World,* London, 1914.

FIFTY YEARS OF EXPLORATION, 1902–1952 *

Lowell Thomas

In 1952 Popular Mechanics invited the versatile and popular writer Lowell Thomas to discuss and describe in non-technical language the major points in the previous 50 years of exploration. The result was the following article, which not only tells what happened but also gives the reader the feel of the various fields of exploration. It shows the rapid progress of twentieth-century achievements, indicating in particular the importance of the new airplane in scouting out regions infinitely more easily and quickly than the old surface methods. It is also interesting in view of the contrast between that progress up to 1952 and the still further achievements in the different fields during the dozen years since that time. There is every prospect that even the present situation of 1964 will be "dated" before long by still further exploring progress.

The Thomas account starts with the story of polar exploration in the half-century, when the long efforts to reach the poles and to traverse the Northeast and Northwest passages suddenly bore fruit. In the Arctic the fact that planes and missiles can travel that shortest route over the top of the earth led later to elaborate permanent bases far above the Arctic Circle to give warning of possible attack. Nuclear submarines, moreover, have been able to traverse the top of the world under the ice, even surfacing at the North Pole. In the Antarctic, which had been only partly explored by 1952, virtually that whole icebound continent has been explored. This was achieved partly through the cooperation of several nations in the International Geophysical Year (IGY) in 1956–1957, in addition to repeated expeditions by the United States Navy. That International Geophysical Year also led to important results in other fields of exploration. In addition there have been remarkable discoveries in the mysteries of the bottom of the sea and other aspects of oceanography since Thomas wrote. The most novel exploration of all—the penetration of outer space—which he mentioned only as a project, has resulted in spectacular progress, as will be indicated in the next section.

---

* Lowell Thomas, "Fifty Years of Exploration," *Popular Mechanics*, August 1952, pp. 94–99. By permission of *Popular Mechanics*.

adequate for the job. I once asked Wilkins the reason for
s novel attempt. His reply: "The captain's teeth!" Know-
ience that intense cold always brings on savage toothache,
d that all his men see their dentists. Only one man failed,
y submerged beneath the icy waters of the Arctic Ocean
the *Nautilus* was in such agony that they were forced to
re reaching their goal.

e greatest boons ever provided to explorers have come out
II, especially in aviation and in the way of clothing and
mer I took time off from my radio work for a journey to
vith the Juneau Ice Field Research Project, sponsored by
Geographical Society, in Alaska. There I participated in
flights from a vast glacier. These were made by C-47s—
-assisted take-offs from the neve surface and over the
50-square-mile ice field. Planes dropped supplies by para-
the icecap. One of the chief purposes of the expedition
of glaciers. Leader Maynard Malcolm Miller and his col-
out cores of glacial ice with an oil rig from several hun-
! These ice cores are fabulous. They're like translucent
as rock. This big expedition, which hopes to continue its
rs, is trying to find out how fast the glaciers are receding.
has much to tell us about the changes in the world's
e gradual warming up of the earth. Without modern ex-
ods, such discoveries would remain locked forever from
ge.

mechanization is spoiling the high adventure of explora-
ong. There is nothing dull about the tale that came out of
ilderness of four Bureau of Reclamation geologists ex-
ver-dam sites in the territory's wild canyons. They were
by helicopter after a series of incredible experiences.
Ade Jaskar, Terrence Robbins, Harry Johnson and their
wanda of Anchorage, set out July 9, 1950, from their base
's Canyon, where they'd been set down by helicopter,
g modern science could supply for comfort and speed.
as aluminum "air skiff" boats (air-lifted to the base camp)
ird motors carried them, their .375 Magnum bear guns,
ent and modern rations into the current of the canyon
lays they pushed, poled and dragged their boats over sand
t shown in the aerial survey they'd made before the trip.
ey'd surveyed two dam sites and finally hit deep water.
f the Tyone River, they picked up their last cache of gaso-
n advance by float plane.

Twelve streamlined Arctic-ized Navy ships slipped out of the
Panama Canal harbor of Balboa one morning in December 1946 and
swung south toward the "White Continent."

This—Rear Adm. Richard E. Byrd's fifth expedition to the Antarctic,
Operation High Jump—was to be "exploration with a difference."
Stowed in the hangar deck of the carrier *Philippine Sea* were a Navy
helicopter and a fleet of the latest landplanes and seaplanes for photo-
mapping the Antarctic icecap. Each plane would carry five cameras—
one pointed straight down, two at an angle of 30 degrees from the horizontal, and two focused on the instruments, one on the clock and the
other on the altimeter. These three-dimensional photos could then be
pieced together to give a perfect map of the icecap, its lofty mountains
and chasms—a detailed map of areas where no human foot had been.

As the fleet edged its way into the first pack ice, the helicopter soared
aloft to act as the "eyes" of the icebreaker *Northwind* leading the cavalcade of ships. A submarine, the *Sennet*, put out into the Southern
Ocean to act as the expedition's mobile radio weather station. Aboard the
ships were some of the latest wartime scientific devices to make life
easier at Little America, base camp on the Bay of Whales. There were
insulated prefabricated houses, Caterpillar tractor snowmobiles, ice
tractors for drawing teams of sleds and a magnetometer—an instrument
for mapping from the air the terrain under the polar ice fields. Personal
comforts included polar clothing, snow goggles, electric blankets and
even Christmas turkeys! "Modern steam-heated exploring," as one observer described it.

I was talking recently to Sir Hubert Wilkins, our top expert on
Arctic clothing, about the special suits. He told me that the Arctic-
equipped serviceman today carries 193 pieces of clothing which weigh
192 pounds! Wilkins' opinion is that the Eskimos were right in the first
place. There is nothing to beat fur and skins. Hence, military researchers
are hunting for a material that will resemble these skins. Their idea is
to use air cells to provide an insulating vapor barrier.

All this is a far cry from the brave navigators who sailed uncharted
seas in search of unexplored continents no more than a few decades ago,
their crews ravaged by sickness, exposure and a diet of salty meat and
moldy biscuits. Or, worse, the foot-slogging expeditions through tropical
rain forests, ravaged by fever and plagued by hunger.

As I walk through the entrance hall of the American Geographical
Society's home in New York, I am always struck by the tremendous advances in exploration since the turn of the century when *Popular Mechanics* made its first appearance. On the walls before me are the names
of illustrious men who have received the awards of the society—Scott,

Shackleton, Peary, Amundsen, Byrd, Wilkins, Roy Chapman Andrews, Ellsworth, D'Abruzzi, to name only a few. There was no steam-heated exploring for these men in their endeavors.

Only a short 50 years ago the greatest ambition of every explorer was to be the first to reach the Poles—via crude sleds, dogs, their own legs and Eskimo clothes for protection. Eight times Robert E. Peary faced the icy winds of that northern waste and was beaten back. In 1909, he set out for his ninth and last try. Peary was 52—by no means young for Arctic exploring—and had lost all but two of his toes from frostbite. On the final leg of the 500-mile sledge trip, he battled fierce, icy gales across the ice. With him was only Matt Henson, his famous Negro companion who had accompanied him on all his previous attempts, and four Eskimos. Henson is an old friend of mine. I once asked him on a broadcast why Peary should have selected him out of all his party for that epic trip? "Why," he said, "I was the only guy who didn't have frozen feet. Peary with his misssing toes was half-frozen all the time!"

On April 6, 1909, they reached their goal—the North Pole conquered at last! The secret of Peary's success was his ability to live as an Eskimo. He built snow igloos, wore Eskimo seal furs and trapped the seals—a real Nanook of the North. Also, he had a team of rugged outdoorsmen like Henson, Donald MacMillan and Bob Bartlett.

As soon as the news of Peary's triumph reached the "outside," the eyes of the world were turned south. Within two years the race for the South Pole was on. It was Capt. Robert Falcon Scott, a British naval officer, who led the first streamlined spearhead into the White Continent. Scott's plans were to roar over the ice with the first motor sledges. Shetland ponies would carry his baggage. His ship, the *Terra Nova*, was loaded with knockdown huts and all the latest scientific gear for conquering the snowy wastes.

At the same time, Roald Amundsen, a Norwegian, was getting set for the same dash. But he followed Peary's example, taking only the simplest equipment—dog teams, skis and sleds.

A year later the tragic story of the race between these two men was told. Scott, with four companions, dogged by misfortune and appalling weather, and dragging their own sledges, reached the Pole to find the Norwegian flag flying above an empty tent. Amundsen, with eight companions on skis, their sledges drawn by dogs, had beaten him by a month. With heavy hearts, the Englishmen turned for their base—800 miles of solid dragging on foot in the face of screaming blizzard. They never made it. Eight months later their bodies were found frozen in a tent nine miles from a supply cache. Beside Scott's body lay his diary

telling the whole poignant story and seems a pity, but I do not think I c

With World War I came enorm Three pioneer flyers in particular provide to the mysteries of the w Byrd and Lincoln Ellsworth. As earl by a Swede, Dr. S. A. Andree, to steered by sails and guide ropes, bu sage buoys from the craft were pick balloon was ever found.

But in April 1926, the *Chantier* Liberty ship fleet, steamed out of N was a Fokker monoplane, the *Josep* Byrd, then a Commander, and his Bay, Spitsbergen, the plane was pu 9, 1926, the two flyers took off an Fifteen and a half hours later they men in history to fly over the Nort

A few days later another Ame Norwegian, Captain Amundsen c Spitsbergen in an airship, the *No* turned to Spitsbergen after reaching kept straight on and, after 72 hours and landed at Teller near Bering

Byrd's No. 1 moment of glory the North Pole flight, he confided was to fly over the South Pole. On J Bay of Whales and christened Litt set up and elaborate equipment, i snowmobile and large stores of foc Antarctic icecap. After reconnoiteri dream came true. He made the fi 1929. At the controls of the three-e Viking, Bernt Balchen.

In some ways the most unust voyage of Sir Hubert Wilkins. An a veteran explorer, Wilkins wante ice in the submarine *Nautilus*. He

[1] The phrase "Liberty Ship" proper of World War II.

old one and i abandoning h ing from expe Wilkins insis and when the the captain o turn back bef

Some of t of World Wa food. Last su the subarctic the American some unusual spectacular je crevasses of a chute to us o was the study leagues gouge dred feet dow glass and har work for 50 y All of which climate and t ploration met man's knowle

If you thir tion, you're w the Alaskan ploring for po finally rescue Daryl Roberts guide, Frank camp at Devi with everythi Two big Doug with big outb survey equipm river. For two bars that hadr By July 13, t At the mouth line, dropped

Then they began to encounter boulders and white water. The rapids boiled faster as they proceeded and drenched them with spray. They stopped often to bail. As the lead boat bearing Roberts and Johnson rounded a bend, it hit three shore-to-shore swells that sent the craft wheeling crazily. The load shifted and in a moment it had capsized. Minutes later the second boat did exactly the same. Gone were their guns and supplies—deep in the heart of unexplored bear country. Choking, they were swept down the rapids clinging to the keels of the upset boats. Roberts and Johnson finally left their rocketing craft and hit for shore. They made it just as the other boat hurtled past, flipped over and whirled in a shallow eddy where Jaskar and Swanda managed to beach it. But Robbins was picked up by the current and carried off. He came ashore several miles downstream after Herculean efforts.

For a week the men, all their supplies and guns gone, lived off the subarctic wilderness and a few items that had washed ashore after the upset—a can of powdered milk, baking powder, a sack of soaked flour, a can of dried eggs, a waterproof container of matches and a tarpaulin. One musette bag contained survey instruments and paper clips. From the latter, Jaskar fashioned fishhooks. They made rods of willow, leaders of bits of blasting wire Swanda had in a pocket, and line pulled from the tarpaulin. They swatted flies for bait. With this gear, they caught 74 fish during their sojurn in the wilderness.

Their distress signal was a series of driftwood poles in the form of an X, with an orange lifejacket placed at each tip. Cooking utensils came from gas and oil cans. They whittled ladles from crate wood and made forks from willow branches. Meanwhile, with their meager supply of instruments, they proceeded to survey near-by Vee Canyon for a dam site.

July 17 had been set as the date for helicopter search in case they hadn't come back. But no helicopter showed. Actually, two pilots of the famous Tenth Rescue Squadron had flown one in, sighted the abandoned boat on a beach and tried to land beside it. But they crashed. Two more men were lost in the wilds. Next day another Tenth Rescue C-47, looking for the lost helicopter, spotted both parties. Another helicopter went out and the entire group came back to civilization intact.

Later in the year, the same group went back to finish the job on Vee Canyon. This time, they went in by helicopter but once again cracked up on landing. They shot birds with their bear guns and lived on a cache of supplies they found in an old prospector's hut until once again they were rescued by helicopter. Dull? Hardly. And as a result of their persistence and courage, Vee Canyon has been proved a feasible site for a power dam which one day may be a key to opening the vast Alaskan wilderness. That's exploring today—the kind that pays off. By the way, the airmen of the Tenth Rescue Squadron have saved some 2000 lives in the past few years since Bernt Balchen organized that fabulous group.

Central Asia

Perhaps one of the most exciting and mysterious regions of the world is Central Asia—that waste of deserts and mountains from Afghanistan and Tibet to the tundra and deserts of Mongolia and Siberia. Roy Chapman Andrews, a young American naturalist, first struck out into the Gobi Desert in 1916, jogging along on his camel with lines of Mongolian ponies bringing up the supplies. The wilderness was so vast, however, he decided on some swifter form of travel. Back in the States, he staggered the exploring world with the announcement that he was going back to follow up his prehistoric discoveries, and do it with automobiles! On all sides he was laughed at—impossible, they said. But young Doctor Andrews was not to be put off by the cynics. In Detroit he met the Dodge Brothers and unfolded his plans for a motor caravan. They liked the idea. Soon Andrews was back in the Gobi, bouncing along in his Dodges. Sure, some of the cars had flats, and others bogged down in the sands, but they were always hauled out. The gamble had paid off big and Andrews returned to America with one of this century's most sensational paleontological discoveries—giant eggs of the dinosaur! Since then automobiles have helped open vast unexplored areas of the world's deserts with those romantic names—the Gobi, the Takla Makhan, the Kalahari, the Sahara, the Atacama and the Arabian (where I went with T. E. Lawrence and Emir Feisal some 36 years ago). Today it seems only a matter of time—and politics—before all these desert lands are completely explored.

Of all the historic parts of the world, Ceneral Asia has always held more fascination for me than any other area. What lies behind the 20,000-foot Himalayan peaks? In the '20s I crossed Baluchistan and Waziristan, and thence to Afghanistan—the first time the Amir of the Afghans had ever allowed his country and people to be filmed. On that expedition Amanullah, King of Kabul and Light of the World, paraded his court and courtiers before our cameras.

It was not until the summer of 1949 that I was able to set out on the trip I had always dreamed of making—across the Himalayas to Tibet and then by caravan over the roof of the world to the capital of the Dalai Lama's hermit kingdom, the fabulous city of Lhasa. It seemed a chance

Twelve streamlined Arctic-ized Navy ships slipped out of the Panama Canal harbor of Balboa one morning in December 1946 and swung south toward the "White Continent."

This—Rear Adm. Richard E. Byrd's fifth expedition to the Antarctic, Operation High Jump—was to be "exploration with a difference." Stowed in the hangar deck of the carrier *Philippine Sea* were a Navy helicopter and a fleet of the latest landplanes and seaplanes for photo-mapping the Antarctic icecap. Each plane would carry five cameras— one pointed straight down, two at an angle of 30 degrees from the horizontal, and two focused on the instruments, one on the clock and the other on the altimeter. These three-dimensional photos could then be pieced together to give a perfect map of the icecap, its lofty mountains and chasms—a detailed map of areas where no human foot had been.

As the fleet edged its way into the first pack ice, the helicopter soared aloft to act as the "eyes" of the icebreaker *Northwind* leading the cavalcade of ships. A submarine, the *Sennet,* put out into the Southern Ocean to act as the expedition's mobile radio weather station. Aboard the ships were some of the latest wartime scientific devices to make life easier at Little America, base camp on the Bay of Whales. There were insulated prefabricated houses, Caterpillar tractor snowmobiles, ice tractors for drawing teams of sleds and a magnetometer—an instrument for mapping from the air the terrain under the polar ice fields. Personal comforts included polar clothing, snow goggles, electric blankets and even Christmas turkeys! "Modern steam-heated exploring," as one observer described it.

I was talking recently to Sir Hubert Wilkins, our top expert on Arctic clothing, about the special suits. He told me that the Arctic-equipped serviceman today carries 193 pieces of clothing which weigh 192 pounds! Wilkins' opinion is that the Eskimos were right in the first place. There is nothing to beat fur and skins. Hence, military researchers are hunting for a material that will resemble these skins. Their idea is to use air cells to provide an insulating vapor barrier.

All this is a far cry from the brave navigators who sailed uncharted seas in search of unexplored continents no more than a few decades ago, their crews ravaged by sickness, exposure and a diet of salty meat and moldy biscuits. Or, worse, the foot-slogging expeditions through tropical rain forests, ravaged by fever and plagued by hunger.

As I walk through the entrance hall of the American Geographical Society's home in New York, I am always struck by the tremendous advances in exploration since the turn of the century when *Popular Mechanics* made its first appearance. On the walls before me are the names of illustrious men who have received the awards of the society—Scott,

Shackleton, Peary, Amundsen, Byrd, Wilkins, Roy Chapman Andrews, Ellsworth, D'Abruzzi, to name only a few. There was no steam-heated exploring for these men in their endeavors.

Only a short 50 years ago the greatest ambition of every explorer was to be the first to reach the Poles—via crude sleds, dogs, their own legs and Eskimo clothes for protection. Eight times Robert E. Peary faced the icy winds of that northern waste and was beaten back. In 1909, he set out for his ninth and last try. Peary was 52—by no means young for Arctic exploring—and had lost all but two of his toes from frostbite. On the final leg of the 500-mile sledge trip, he battled fierce, icy gales across the ice. With him was only Matt Henson, his famous Negro companion who had accompanied him on all his previous attempts, and four Eskimos. Henson is an old friend of mine. I once asked him on a broadcast why Peary should have selected him out of all his party for that epic trip? "Why," he said, "I was the only guy who didn't have frozen feet. Peary with his misssing toes was half-frozen all the time!"

On April 6, 1909, they reached their goal—the North Pole conquered at last! The secret of Peary's success was his ability to live as an Eskimo. He built snow igloos, wore Eskimo seal furs and trapped the seals—a real Nanook of the North. Also, he had a team of rugged outdoorsmen like Henson, Donald MacMillan and Bob Bartlett.

As soon as the news of Peary's triumph reached the "outside," the eyes of the world were turned south. Within two years the race for the South Pole was on. It was Capt. Robert Falcon Scott, a British naval officer, who led the first streamlined spearhead into the White Continent. Scott's plans were to roar over the ice with the first motor sledges. Shetland ponies would carry his baggage. His ship, the *Terra Nova*, was loaded with knockdown huts and all the latest scientific gear for conquering the snowy wastes.

At the same time, Roald Amundsen, a Norwegian, was getting set for the same dash. But he followed Peary's example, taking only the simplest equipment—dog teams, skis and sleds.

A year later the tragic story of the race between these two men was told. Scott, with four companions, dogged by misfortune and appalling weather, and dragging their own sledges, reached the Pole to find the Norwegian flag flying above an empty tent. Amundsen, with eight companions on skis, their sledges drawn by dogs, had beaten him by a month. With heavy hearts, the Englishmen turned for their base—800 miles of solid dragging on foot in the face of screaming blizzard. They never made it. Eight months later their bodies were found frozen in a tent nine miles from a supply cache. Beside Scott's body lay his diary telling the whole poignant story and ending with the heroic words: "It seems a pity, but I do not think I can write more."

With World War I came enormous strides in the field of aviation. Three pioneer flyers in particular saw the key that airplane would provide to the mysteries of the world—Sir Hubert Wilkins, Admiral Byrd and Lincoln Ellsworth. As early as 1897 an attempt had been made by a Swede, Dr. S. A. Andree, to fly to the North Pole in a balloon steered by sails and guide ropes, but this ended in tragedy. Empty message buoys from the craft were picked up years later—but no sign of the balloon was ever found.

But in April 1926, the *Chantier,* a relic of the World War I wooden Liberty ship fleet, steamed out of New York harbor.[1] Stowed in her hold was a Fokker monoplane, the *Josephine Ford,* and aboard were Admiral Byrd, then a Commander, and his navigator Floyd Bennett. At King's Bay, Spitsbergen, the plane was put ashore. Just after midnight on May 9, 1926, the two flyers took off and headed north in perfect weather. Fifteen and a half hours later they were back in Spitsbergen—the first men in history to fly over the North Pole.

A few days later another American, Lincoln Ellsworth, with the Norwegian, Captain Amundsen of South Pole fame, took off from Spitsbergen in an airship, the *Norge.* Whereas Byrd on his flight returned to Spitsbergen after reaching the Pole, Amundsen and Ellsworth kept straight on and, after 72 hours in the air, sighted the coast of Alaska and landed at Teller near Bering Strait.

Byrd's No. 1 moment of glory was still to come. Immediately after the North Pole flight, he confided to Amundsen that his next ambition was to fly over the South Pole. On Jan. 1, 1929, a base was chosen on the Bay of Whales and christened Little America. A radio station was soon set up and elaborate equipment, including five planes, husky dogs, a snowmobile and large stores of food and clothing, were landed on the Antarctic icecap. After reconnoitering up the Liv Glacier Canyon, Byrd's dream came true. He made the first flight over the Pole—on Nov. 28, 1929. At the controls of the three-engine Ford monoplane was a modern Viking, Bernt Balchen.

In some ways the most unusual polar attempt was the undersea voyage of Sir Hubert Wilkins. An aviator of worldwide experience and a veteran explorer, Wilkins wanted to reach the North Pole under the ice in the submarine *Nautilus.* He failed largely because the sub was an

[1] The phrase "Liberty Ship" properly belonged to the later emergency ships of World War II.

old one and inadequate for the job. I once asked Wilkins the reason for abandoning his novel attempt. His reply: "The captain's teeth!" Knowing from experience that intense cold always brings on savage toothache, Wilkins insisted that all his men see their dentists. Only one man failed, and when they submerged beneath the icy waters of the Arctic Ocean the captain of the *Nautilus* was in such agony that they were forced to turn back before reaching their goal.

Some of the greatest boons ever provided to explorers have come out of World War II, especially in aviation and in the way of clothing and food. Last summer I took time off from my radio work for a journey to the subarctic with the Juneau Ice Field Research Project, sponsored by the American Geographical Society, in Alaska. There I participated in some unusual flights from a vast glacier. These were made by C-47s—spectacular jet-assisted take-offs from the neve surface and over the crevasses of a 750-square-mile ice field. Planes dropped supplies by parachute to us on the icecap. One of the chief purposes of the expedition was the study of glaciers. Leader Maynard Malcolm Miller and his colleagues gouged out cores of glacial ice with an oil rig from several hundred feet down! These ice cores are fabulous. They're like translucent glass and hard as rock. This big expedition,which hopes to continue its work for 50 years, is trying to find out how fast the glaciers are receding. All of which has much to tell us about the changes in the world's climate and the gradual warming up of the earth. Without modern exploration methods, such discoveries would remain locked forever from man's knowledge.

If you think mechanization is spoiling the high adventure of exploration, you're wrong. There is nothing dull about the tale that came out of the Alaskan wilderness of four Bureau of Reclamation geologists exploring for power-dam sites in the territory's wild canyons. They were finally rescued by helicopter after a series of incredible experiences. Daryl Roberts, Ade Jaskar, Terrence Robbins, Harry Johnson and their guide, Frank Swanda of Anchorage, set out July 9, 1950, from their base camp at Devil's Canyon, where they'd been set down by helicopter, with everything modern science could supply for comfort and speed. Two big Douglas aluminum "air skiff" boats (air-lifted to the base camp) with big outboard motors carried them, their .375 Magnum bear guns, survey equipment and modern rations into the current of the canyon river. For two days they pushed, poled and dragged their boats over sand bars that hadn't shown in the aerial survey they'd made before the trip. By July 13, they'd surveyed two dam sites and finally hit deep water. At the mouth of the Tyone River, they picked up their last cache of gasoline, dropped in advance by float plane.

Then they began to encounter boulders and white water. The rapids boiled faster as they proceeded and drenched them with spray. They stopped often to bail. As the lead boat bearing Roberts and Johnson rounded a bend, it hit three shore-to-shore swells that sent the craft wheeling crazily. The load shifted and in a moment it had capsized. Minutes later the second boat did exactly the same. Gone were their guns and supplies—deep in the heart of unexplored bear country. Choking, they were swept down the rapids clinging to the keels of the upset boats. Roberts and Johnson finally left their rocketing craft and hit for shore. They made it just as the other boat hurtled past, flipped over and whirled in a shallow eddy where Jaskar and Swanda managed to beach it. But Robbins was picked up by the current and carried off. He came ashore several miles downstream after Herculean efforts.

For a week the men, all their supplies and guns gone, lived off the subarctic wilderness and a few items that had washed ashore after the upset—a can of powdered milk, baking powder, a sack of soaked flour, a can of dried eggs, a waterproof container of matches and a tarpaulin. One musette bag contained survey instruments and paper clips. From the latter, Jaskar fashioned fishhooks. They made rods of willow, leaders of bits of blasting wire Swanda had in a pocket, and line pulled from the tarpaulin. They swatted flies for bait. With this gear, they caught 74 fish during their sojourn in the wilderness.

Their distress signal was a series of driftwood poles in the form of an X, with an orange lifejacket placed at each tip. Cooking utensils came from gas and oil cans. They whittled ladles from crate wood and made forks from willow branches. Meanwhile, with their meager supply of instruments, they proceeded to survey near-by Vee Canyon for a dam site.

July 17 had been set as the date for helicopter search in case they hadn't come back. But no helicopter showed. Actually, two pilots of the famous Tenth Rescue Squadron had flown one in, sighted the abandoned boat on a beach and tried to land beside it. But they crashed. Two more men were lost in the wilds. Next day another Tenth Rescue C-47, looking for the lost helicopter, spotted both parties. Another helicopter went out and the entire group came back to civilization intact.

Later in the year, the same group went back to finish the job on Vee Canyon. This time, they went in by helicopter but once again cracked up on landing. They shot birds with their bear guns and lived on a cache of supplies they found in an old prospector's hut until once again they were rescued by helicopter. Dull? Hardly. And as a result of their persistence and courage, Vee Canyon has been proved a feasible site for a power dam which one day may be a key to opening the vast Alaskan wilderness. That's exploring today—the kind that pays off. By the way, the airmen of the Tenth Rescue Squadron have saved some 2000 lives in the past few years since Bernt Balchen organized that fabulous group.

Central Asia

Perhaps one of the most exciting and mysterious regions of the world is Central Asia—that waste of deserts and mountains from Afghanistan and Tibet to the tundra and deserts of Mongolia and Siberia. Roy Chapman Andrews, a young American naturalist, first struck out into the Gobi Desert in 1916, jogging along on his camel with lines of Mongolian ponies bringing up the supplies. The wilderness was so vast, however, he decided on some swifter form of travel. Back in the States, he staggered the exploring world with the announcement that he was going back to follow up his prehistoric discoveries, and do it with automobiles! On all sides he was laughed at—impossible, they said. But young Doctor Andrews was not to be put off by the cynics. In Detroit he met the Dodge Brothers and unfolded his plans for a motor caravan. They liked the idea. Soon Andrews was back in the Gobi, bouncing along in his Dodges. Sure, some of the cars had flats, and others bogged down in the sands, but they were always hauled out. The gamble had paid off big and Andrews returned to America with one of this century's most sensational paleontological discoveries—giant eggs of the dinosaur! Since then automobiles have helped open vast unexplored areas of the world's deserts with those romantic names—the Gobi, the Takla Makhan, the Kalahari, the Sahara, the Atacama and the Arabian (where I went with T. E. Lawrence and Emir Feisal some 36 years ago). Today it seems only a matter of time—and politics—before all these desert lands are completely explored.

Of all the historic parts of the world, Ceneral Asia has always held more fascination for me than any other area. What lies behind the 20,000-foot Himalayan peaks? In the '20s I crossed Baluchistan and Waziristan, and thence to Afghanistan—the first time the Amir of the Afghans had ever allowed his country and people to be filmed. On that expedition Amanullah, King of Kabul and Light of the World, paraded his court and courtiers before our cameras.

It was not until the summer of 1949 that I was able to set out on the trip I had always dreamed of making—across the Himalayas to Tibet and then by caravan over the roof of the world to the capital of the Dalai Lama's hermit kingdom, the fabulous city of Lhasa. It seemed a chance in a million when permission came through for Lowell, Jr., and me to make the "forbidden journey." Again, of course, we had our cameras and were able to bring back a color film of those strange and mysterious people in a land where a fourth of all males are monks and lamas. We visited and photographed the Dalai Lama's palace—the Potala, nearly as high as the Empire State Building—and Drepung—largest monastery in the world, home of 10,000 monks—in a highly civilized country where there isn't a wheel, except a prayer wheel.

Although we covered well-trodden caravan trails across the 17,000-foot passes to the Forbidden City, one innovation we can lay claim to was the first use of radio recording. We sent back to CBS a complete account of our progress across the Himalayas and our near-tragic return journey to India—when my horse hurled me down onto a boulder and broke my hip in eight places, on a lofty and remote pass far from any medical aid.

South America

The past 50 years have provided some of the most exciting adventure and mystery stories in the history of exploration. A perennial newspaper headline is the "Discovery of Colonel Fawcett." Endless travelers claim to have seen or heard of Fawcett alive in the wilds of South America—and I seem to have had a share of the stories on my broadcasts, too! In 1925, Col. Percy Fawcett, an Englishman, went into the jungles of Brazil's Matto Grosso to look for the ruins of a lost civilization.

During mapping expeditions in Bolivia, Peru and Brazil, Fawcett heard tales of a forgotten race of white Indians. Intrigued by the idea that these might be old Inca survivors of El Dorado, the mythical City of Gold, Fawcett persuaded the Royal Geographical Society in London to help him finance an expedition. On May 20, 1925, a report was sent by the expedition from deep in the Matto Grosso saying that they were heading into the Indian country beyond the Rio das Mortes—the River of Death. After that—no more. It was not until two years later that rumors began to circulate about the fate of Colonel Fawcett and his son. Rescue expeditions set out but the jungle never gave up the secret of the lost seekers of El Dorado. Last spring the Brazilian government proudly announced that it had cleared up the mystery by finding the bones of Colonel Fawcett. It now appears, however, that the jawbone was not that of the colonel, or so says his London dentist. Late in summer while in Brazil, I discussed this with South American explorers—two priests who had just walked in and flown out of the same unknown. It took them 80 days on foot to reach the nearest settlement where a plane could pick them up. They were still optimistic that the Fawcett mystery will be solved.

Much of the Amazon basin—that vast confusion of swamps and jungle where huge anaconda snakes, electric eels, sting rays, alligators and flesh-eating piranha fish lie in wait for the unwary—is still largely a blank on our maps. Today, an Anglo-American expedition is high in the Andes of Peru searching for the source of the river.

No matter what happens to exploration, people will always debate the question, "Who got there first?" Right now there's a squabble in the making over the discovery of the Orinoco. Recently a party of French scientists led by a Venezuelan, a Doctor Cruxent, claimed to have reached the true headwaters after hacking their way through dense jungle and the gorges of the Sierra Parima. They were blazing a trail first sought in 1618 by Sir Walter Raleigh. Their claim came back by radio and the newspapers were full of the dramatic feat. But here's the twister. Another expedition headed by an American, Dr. Herbert S. Dickey, now claims that they already had been there in 1931. Doctor Dickey, an entomologist, and one of my colleagues of the Explorers Club, says that he was hunting for natives to act as sculpture models and reached Tama Tama at the river's source in Brazil on July 28, 1931, more than 20 years ago. So now the barbed words will fly again.

Perhaps our generation may be the last of terrestrial explorers, or nearly so. Already exploring is becoming three-dimensional—into the oceans, the skies, icecaps and the bowels of the earth. We need scientific investigation of weather conditions, glaciology, more meteorology and an urgent search for more oil and rare minerals such as uranium. Though less than half the earth's surface actually has been surveyed, geographers using airplanes and helicopters will be able, fairly easily, to fill in the gaps in Africa and South America and in New Guinea, Arabia, Central Asia and Alaska. Then there is still two-thirds of Antarctica that remains unseen by human eye. Modern equipment and techniques—the air drop, the helicopter, guided missiles, the bulldozer, wonder drugs, the jet plane—all provide help in key with the fast tempo of our time for the modern explorer, help undreamed of 50 years ago. Television, too, for already they are lowering a special TV-camera bathoscope into the nethermost depths of the ocean.

Further research into existing data is moving fast. One phase of this work is the idea under study by the armed services of using moving ice floes as landing fields on the Polar Ocean. This scheme was developed at first by a Russian explorer, Ivan Papanin, who in 1937 set up a camp on the ice at the North Pole and subsequently drifted over a thousand miles on an ice floe before being rescued nine months later off the east coast of Greenland. Since then our own airmen have spent a great deal of time on the ice floes of the Polar Sea.

With all this speed of discovery, you may wonder what will be left to explore in 50 years. Plenty!

Since Plato told the story of a lost submerged continent, Atlantis, men have wondered about the mysteries of the mountains and valleys of the ocean. In spite of the great strides made in oceanographic work with echo-sounding and other electronic devices, w still have only the sketchiest knowledge of the topography of the ocean depths and of its inhabitants. Nearly three quarters of our planet is covered by water—dark, silent, at enormous pressure and undisturbed since the beginning of time.

As far as I know, only two men have ever even entered this region of mystery—Dr. William Beebe and Otis Barton. Knowing that no diving suit could withstand the pressure a half mile down (over 1100 pounds to the square inch) Beebe and Barton designed a steel ball, known as a bathysphere, for their first descents off the Bermudian isle of Nonsuch. The bathysphere was built of 1½-inch steel with fused quartz windows and was equipped with a two-way telephone line and power lines for a searchlight. The question of air supply was solved by the use of oxygen tanks with chemicals to absorb the moisture and expended air. Manned by the two scientists, the steel globe was lowered to a depth of 3028 feet in the ocean off Bermuda and the searchlight was switched on. Before their eyes was revealed a parade of horrific and grotesquely shaped fish and crustaceans. Since then Barton designed a new sphere, the bathoscope, and in the summer of 1949 descended still farther, to 4500 feet in the Pacific off the coast of California. As Beebe summed it up after one of his dives: "The only other place comparable to these marvelous nether regions must surely be naked space itself, out far beyond the atmosphere—where the blackness of space, the shining planets, comets, suns and stars must really be closely akin to the world of life as it appears to the eyes of an awed human being, in the open ocean, one half mile down."

To the reader of 1900, the idea of a visit to the moon was just a Wellsian fantasy, but much that Jules Verne and Wells predicted is now history. *Around the World in Eighty Days* has been reduced to "Around the World in Less than Eight Days." Already scientists are talking seriously about trips to the moon, and even to Mars and Venus, aboard atomic-powered rocket ships. Outer-space exploration may well be the big field for tomorrow's young scientists. Today we are preparing the way for it. [1952].

.   .   .   .

Until then, there will be plenty of work for explorers right here on our tiny piece of space. In spite of the fact that few "white spots" are left to plant a flag on, we keep finding new things in our own uncharted wilderness.

Last year alone, scores of expeditions came back with libraries of new knowledge. On the Caspian Sea in Iran, the bones of three Stone Age persons were found in a cave where the roof dropped on them 75,000 years ago. In Iraq, busy archeologists uncovered a 7000-year-old town, oldest known to exist, even older than Ur of the Chaldees. Its age was pin-pointed by radioactive-carbon measurement, an atomic-age measuring boon to scientists that is revolutionizing this kind of work.

Across the burning sands of Arabia's Rub Al Khali desert, explorers are talking of what they think may have been the Queen of Sheba's ancient city—a ruined city of alabaster temples and palaces in the desert sands of Mareb, in Yemen.

Exploring scientists also learned that the huge Chubb crater in northern Quebec is the biggest hole ever left by a meteor.

Surprises keep turning up. On a previously unexplored island near Bermuda, ornithologists found living cahows—ocean birds believed extinct for 300 years. Oceanographers discovered undersea mountains 11,000 feet high near the Orkney Islands. They also found life existing six miles under the sea in the Johnson Deep off the Philippines.

We could go on for pages just naming the exploration feats of 1951. And the chances are that when the year 2000 rolls around, we still will only have scratched the surface of Mother Earth's secrets. No matter what happens, there will always be room for good scientific explorers— men whose curiosity about this world in which we dwell won't let them sit by the fireside any longer than it takes to tell the folks back home about their last trek "beyond the utmost purple rim."

NOTES

Terence Armstrong, *The Northern Sea Route: Russian Exploitation of the North East Passage,* Cambridge, Eng., 1952.

John E. Caswell, *Arctic Frontiers,* Norman, Okla., 1957.

Robert C. Cowen, *Frontiers of the Sea: The Story of Oceanographic Exploration,* Garden City, 1960.

Nellis M. Crouse, *In Quest of the Western Ocean*, 1938; *The Search for the North Pole*, New York, 1947.

Frank Debenham, *Antarctica: The Story of a Continent*, New York, 1961.

Ernest S. Dodge, *Northwest by Sea*, New York, 1961.

George J. Dufek, *Operation Deepfreeze*, New York, 1957.

Norman Kemp, *Conquest of the Antarctic*, New York, 1957.

THE EXPLORATION OF OUTER SPACE *

Harrison Brown

Not content with exploring the whole surface of the earth and the bottom of the sea, men began, shortly after the end of World War II, to explore the mysteries of outer space, which begins several hundred miles beyond the atmosphere surrounding the earth and extends indefinitely out into the universe. For years, boys had thrilled at the exploits of Buck Rogers and other heroes of science fiction, but only now did the scientists and technologists begin to convert those fantasies into reality.

The initial stimulus came from the Germans, with their development of powerful rocket propulsion during World War II. The continuing progress, however, was in no small part a product of the cold war, with the United States and Russia engaging in expensive rivalry, partly as a matter of world prestige. The Americans had considered themselves far ahead of the Russians in scientific and technological progress. It was consequently a severe shock to their complacency when the Russians, in October 1957, put their pioneer Sputnik satellite into orbit, circling the earth. The first American satellite followed ten weeks later. The Russians also took the lead in manned space flight, sending a hardy astronaut into orbit. Early in 1962 the first American followed suit, after others had made shorter space flights. Those flights, both manned and unmanned, yielded much knowledge about the nature of radiation and other aspects of outer space. Space satellites also made possible new techniques in communication.

Along with the continued orbiting of the earth by scores of different satellites have gone still more ambitious projects to reach the moon and

* Harrison Brown, in "A Symposium on Space," *The Great Ideas Today*, 1963 (Robert M. Hutchins and Mortimer J. Adler, eds.) (Chicago: Encyclopaedia Britannica, 1963), pp. 61–73. By permission of *The Great Ideas Today*.

some of the planets. The Russians again took the lead, and were able to photograph the far side of the moon, with the Americans following later. Less successful were the efforts to reach the planet Venus at a time when it was closer than usual to the earth. It has been planned to send astronauts to the moon as a start, and then possibly still further distant.

The cost of these space programs has run into billions, and there are skeptics who can foresee little tangible value from such activity and feel that those huge sums could be spent to greater advantage. The prospective problems and advantages of such programs are discussed in the following article by Harrison Brown, one of America's leading physical scientists, who was one of the directors of the atomic research center at Oak Ridge, Tennessee, and later a member of the California Institute of Technology faculty. This was his portion of a symposium of experts on aspects of the space program.

Man appeared on the earth about a million years ago. Though his technological competence has grown steadily, he has been restricted to the earth during all of that time. Now, in our generation, he has developed the competence to fly to the moon and the planets, to observe and study them at first hand. Immense new vistas have been opened to him. He can now learn things which before seemed destined to remain permanently beyond his grasp. This is a prospect which should excite everyone. Those who are not stirred by the thought of man's traveling to the planets are either devoid of curiosity or lack a sense of human destiny. The realization that we may now have it in our power to answer the question of extra-terrestrial life should in itself be sufficent to spur us on.

Throughout his history, man has pursued knowledge in large part because of its utilitarian value: it helps him to master nature. When we examine the research which is being done today, we find that the greater part of it is aimed at the achievement of practical goals: to win wars, to prolong life, to make money. It is understandable that such research is undertaken, and it is often enormously sophisticated. Yet, in a moral sense, such research is scarcely above the animal level. It is simply an attempt to extend our ancient predatory capabilities and to create protective devices of increased efficiency against predators.

However, there have always been some men who have held that the pursuit of knowledge for its own sake is one of man's most noble characteristics and the one which most distinguishes him from the lower animals. Not to pursue the exploration of space, when it is possible, would therefore be a denial by man of one of his most important attributes. Not to venture to the planets would be a negation of one of life's most noble purposes—understanding ourselves and our origins.

Before we can rationally discuss the value of programs aimed at sending men and instruments into outer space, it is essential that we understand the kinds of problems which such programs might help solve. One of the most important of these problems is that of the origin and evolution of our solar system.

Although man, until very recently, has been earthbound, he has nevertheless succeeded in learning a great deal about our solar system. Using telescopes and other instruments, he has measured the sizes of planets and their satellites. He has learned something about the chemical compositions and temperatures of planetary atmospheres. By subjecting fragments of interplanetary matter which fall upon the earth (meteorites) to intensive chemical and physical examination, he has learned something about the distribution of elements in cosmic matter. He has even been able to determine quite accurately the time at which the earth and meteorites were formed. Naturally, he possesses considerably more information about the earth than he does about other planets, for he has been able to observe it at much closer range.

The major facts which have been accumulated, and which any general theory of the origin of the solar system must explain, fall into a most interesting pattern. It has become evident that there are two distinct groups of planets. The four planets close to the sun are *small*: Mercury, Venus, Earth, and Mars. Those farther away from the sun are very *large*: Jupiter, Saturn, Uranus, and Neptune. The small inner planets are characterized by high average densities and must therefore be composed primarily of heavy substances such as metal and rock. The large outer planets, by contrast are characterized by very low densities and must therefore be composed primarily of very light, indeed gaseous, substances. Saturn, for example, could float in water. The predominant materials in Jupiter appear to be hydrogen, helium, methane, ammonia, and water.

The atmospheres of the two groups of planets differ dramatically from each other. Mercury is too small and too warm to retain an atmosphere, but the atmospheres of Venus, Earth, and Mars contain substantial, although differing, quantities of carbon dioxide. By contrast, the carbon which exists in the atmospheres of the large outer planets appears to be primarily in the form of methane. There is a similar difference between the forms in which nitrogen is found in the two groups. The nitrogen in the earth's atmosphere is in the form of nitrogen gas, while the nitrogen in the atmosphere of Jupiter is primarily in the form of ammonia. In other words, the atmospheres of the inner planets are chemically oxidized; those of the outer planets are chemically reduced.

Traveling around the sun, then, we see different kinds of bodies. Why are some large and others small? Why are some dense and others "fluffy"? Why are some chemically oxidized and others reduced? At present, we do not have definite answers to these questions, but we have been able to fit the observed facts into a broad picture which seems clear in outline, if not in detail.

The elements which constitute our solar system appear to have been formed about five thousand million years ago as the result of a sequence of nuclear reactions which as yet are not clearly understood. About 4,500 million years ago the newly formed elements and their compounds began to condense, and the processes of planet formation were started. Many chemical compounds were present in this primordial matter, but those which predominated were hydrogen and helium. To a lesser extent, quantities of methane, ammonia, and water were present. Considerably less abundant were the substances which make up the greater part of the earth—silicates and metals.

Condensation processes took place in a gaseous cloud surrounding the primitive sun. Within the asteroid belt, which lies between Mars and Jupiter, the temperatures were sufficiently high to permit the condensation only of the less volatile materials, which were present in but small quantity. Beyond the asteroid belt, however, the more abundant substances such as water, ammonia, and methane condensed. The condensed solids amalgamated by accretion processes and gave rise to planets which, inside the asteroid belt, were composed almost entirely of rock-like material and metals. Outside the asteroid belt, the accretion processes led to the formation of planets composed in large part of methane, ammonia, and water. In the special cases of Jupiter and Saturn, which were particularly favorably situated, large quantities of hydrogen and helium were also retained as the result of gravitational pull.

We know that inside the asteroid belt no substance which was present as a gas at the time of planet formation could have been retained by a planet in appreciable quantity. In other words, none of the inner planets originally possessed atmospheres or oceans. Those which we observe today must be almost entirely of secondary origin. Yet, on the earth we observed huge oceans. If water could not have been retained in free form originally, from where did it come?

The answer appears to be that water was retained originally on the earth chemically bound within the rock-forming silicates. As the earth heated, as the result of gravitational contraction coupled with the liberation of energy stored in radioactive substances, water was liberated from the depths, and oceans were formed. Other gaseous substances were also released by this heating process, in particular methane and other hydro-carbons and ammonia.

The stage was thus set on the earth for a sequence of chemical steps leading to the buildup of carbon compounds of increasing complexity, and eventually to the evolution of molecules which could reproduce themselves. Life emerged, and the resultant living substances began to traverse the long and complicated path which we call evolution.

In the meantime, the flux of radiant energy which fell continually upon the earth gave rise to other chemical processes. In particular, it decomposed atmospheric water vapor into hydrogen and oxygen gases. Because of its lightness, a great deal of the hydrogen escaped from the earth's gravitational pull. The oxygen, which was left behind, combined with carbon compounds to form carbon dioxide and with nitrogen com-pounds to form free nitrogen. Over a period of time, the greater part of the carbon was converted by these processes into carbon dioxide, which combined with calcium in the ocean and was eventually deposited as limestone. A delicate balance was established among the carbon dioxide in the atmosphere, that in the ocean, and that tied up in sedimentary rocks.

Eventually, the primitive living substances learned to "feed" upon the carbon dioxide of the oceans and the atmosphere, making use of the steady flow of radiation from the sun. Photosynthesis was "invented" and made possible the continuation of life processes for an indefinitely long period of time on a stable basis.

Within the thin film of life which covered the earth, there was cease-less pulsation. New species of living matter arose and old ones dis-appeared. Organisms of increasing complexity emerged: single-celled animals, multi-celled animals, animals with supporting structures (bones), vertebrates, fish with lungs, amphibians, reptiles, mammals. Eventually, and recently, man emerged—a creature possessing the power of conceptual thought, a creature which, for the first time in evolution-ary history, could wonder about its past, its origins, and its place in the universe.

What about the other planets? Could life have emerged upon them as well? The emergence of life would seem to call for conditions of "chemical flexibility"—conditions in which a multiplicity of chemical reactions can take place and in which very complicated compounds are stable over long periods of time. It is difficult to imagine life on Nep-tune, for example, because the surface temperature is so low that rates of chemical reactions are extremely slow. It is equally difficult to imagine life on Mercury, where there is no atmosphere and where the tempera-ture of the hot side is so high that complex organic substances would be unstable. Between these two extremes, however, there should be a broad spectrum of conditions in which life might have emerged and flourished.

One might expect *a priori* that Venus, which is about the same size as the earth, would provide conditions suitable for the nourishment of life processes. Study of the planet indicates, however, that although carbon dioxide is extremely abundant in the atmosphere, little if any water is present. Further, the temperature of the planet appears to be so high that any oceans would be vaporized. Under the circumstances, it seems dubious that life exists there today, although it might well have existed at some time in the distant past.

Why should Venus have an oxidized atmosphere and at the same time possess little if any water? It is possible that, since Venus was formed closer to the sun than was the earth, its chemical combinations of water with silicates were less stable, with the result that Venus started its life with a paucity of water. Further, the radiation intensity in the neighborhood of Venus would decompose water at a greater rate than terrestrial water was decomposed, with the result that virtually all water on the planet disappeared.

The situation with respect to Mars is quite different. Although the planet possesses no oceans, water appears to be present. The polar caps show seasonal changes in size, and, on occasion, deposits of hoarfrost can be seen during the Martian dawn. Also, there are color changes on the surface of the planet which appear to be seasonal and which might well be indicative of the presence of some form of plant life. If such life exists, however, it must be able to survive under extremely rugged circumstances. Winter and nighttime temperatures appear to fall far below those of our own Arctic regions, and Martian midday summer heat might be the equivalent of a cold fall day in New England.

It is interesting to speculate as to why Mars possesses so little water. By contrast with Venus, the planet was formed so far from the sun that hydrated rock substances should have been quite stable. It may be that, because of the smallness of the planet, the water was never liberated from the interior. It may also be that water was liberated, but because of the low gravitational pull of the planet, the water has escaped over the ages until it has by now virtually disappeared. If the latter is true, Mars at one time may have had much more water than we see today—indeed the planet may even have had oceans. Under such circumstances, climatic conditions would have been quite different (more moderate) from those we now observe.

With this background of information and speculation, we can state one of the great unsolved problems concerning our universe as follows: Given a planet that possesses "chemical flexibility," what is the probability that life will emerge as the natural end product of a sequence of chemical events? Given a planet that is not too small (like the moon), not too hot (like Mercury), not too cold (like Neptune), not too large (like Jupiter), what is the likelihood that a sequence of chemical steps will result in the emergence, over a period of time, of living substance? Looking at the earth alone, we cannot tell. For all we know, life might be a miracle, and indeed there are many who believe that it is. But if, through space exploration, we were to find life on Venus or Mars or both, it would then appear likely that the probability of life emerging naturally, given adequate conditions, would be as high.

Such a discovery would have profound philosophical importance. We have good reason to believe that planetary systems are fairly abundant in our visible universe—indeed, perhaps as many as a billion billion stars which can be seen through our largest telescopes may have planets traveling about them in orbit. Even if only a small fraction of these were situated in such a way that they were not too close to their stars, not too far away, not too hot, not too cold, not too large, not too small, life could still be a very abundant commodity in our universe. Indeed, were we to find that life of some sort exists on Mars, the likelihood would be high that life also exists on perhaps as many as a thousand billion planets in our visible universe.

This, then, is the broad picture as it appears at the present time. Much of it is fact. A great deal is theory. Much is speculation. The picture is based upon facts gained through intensive study of the earth by men who have been confined to its surface, and by intensive study of the moon and planets from a great distance, using telescopes.

Although there is a great deal which can yet be learned about the planets using terrestrially based equipment, we can see the beginning of the end. Telescopes have limited usefulness. There are certain kinds of important planetary measurements which simply cannot be made from the earth. Indeed, were it not possible to journey to the planets, there would be many questions which would remain unanswered for all time. And of these questions, perhaps the most important is that of extra-terrestrial life. Is the earth unique? Or is life abundant elsewhere?

Our newly developed capabilities of sending spacecraft out of the earth's gravitational field will make it possible for us greatly to increase our understanding of the solar system and its origins. Already vehicles have struck the moon and have come close to Venus and Mars. Given enough effort, it should be possible to land men on the moon and to bring them back safely. With still more effort, it should be possible to send men to Mars and Venus and to bring them back.

Much of what we wish to know about the moon and planets can be learned with instruments. It is not necessary to send men to the moon or to Mars in order to obtain most of the important information which we need concerning these bodies. Indeed, for most purposes instruments are actually more effective than man, and coupled with this, they need not be returned to the earth. The information obtained by instruments can be telemetered back.

Because the moon is so much closer to the earth than are the planets, it will, of course, be our first object of study. Using television cameras, we can obtain, even with a "crash landing," highly detailed pictures of the lunar surface. At present, our very best pictures of the moon have a resolution of about one-half mile. Using a television camera mounted on a lunar probe, a resolution of a few feet should be possible. By using television cameras placed in a spacecraft in orbit about the moon, it should be possible to obtain detailed maps of the entire lunar surface. Other exciting experiments could be undertaken from such a spacecraft. The temperatures of specific areas could be measured accurately. The radioactivity of the lunar surface could be determined, and this would tell us a great deal about is chemical composition. The mass and mass distribution within the moon could be determined accurately.

With improved techniques of rocketry, it should be possible to land a probe upon the moon "softly." This would make possible a variety of important measurements. Truly detailed pictures could be obtained of the region in the vicinity of the landing. The chemical composition of the lunar crust could be determined precisely. One could determine whether or not there are "moonquakes." A variety of other important chemical and physical parameters could be measured which, taken together, would tell us much more that we now know concerning the moon's origin and history—particularly if measurements were made at a number of lunar locations. With further improvement in rocketry techniques, it should be possible to obtain samples of the lunar surface by remote control and to return them to the earth for still more detailed study.

Present techniques of rocketry permit us to launch spacecraft which can come very close to our nearest planetary neighbors—Mars and Venus. The great distances involved restrict the kinds of measurements which can be made, in part because of the increased difficulty of communication. Nevertheless, important measurements can be made, even at present. Television observations can be made, the chemical compositions of the atmospheres can be determined, and other important parameters such as magnetic fields and temperature can be measured.

We will be able to land instrument packages "softly" on Mars and

Venus long before we are able to send men there and bring them back. This will mean that prior to the first human visits to these planets we should have a fairly clear picture of the conditions the visitors will encounter. Detailed television pictures can be transmitted back to the earth. The compositions of the atmospheres can be determined in detail. General climatic conditions can be followed over long periods of time. The surfaces of the planets can be observed through both microscopes and telescopes.

Lower forms of life, corresponding to terrestrial bacteria, can be searched for on Mars and Venus by culturing the material on the surface and examining the cultures with microscopes which are remotely controlled. Higher life forms can be searched for by using television and listening for sounds. Long before the first human visitors reach Mars and Venus, we should have a clear picture as to whether or not life in some form exists on these planets.

If so much can be learned about planets by using instruments, why then do we place so much effort on the manned-space-flight program? The U. S. budget for fiscal year 1963 calls for two-thirds of the total space effort to be placed on the manned-space-flight program while less than one-sixth of the total budget is for scientific research in space. Is this a reasonable distribution?

The fact is that there are few situations involving scientific measurements in which machines are not more effective than men. What, for example, in an orbiting earth satellite, could a man learn that could not be learned with proper instrumentation? The answer is: very little. To this must be added the fact that when we place human beings in orbit, enormous and expensive safety precautions are necessary. We can take a much greater risk with the life of an instrument.

The situation with respect to space is similar to that with respect to the oceans. Most of our knowledge concerning the ocean depths has been obtained using instruments and measuring and sampling devices of various sorts which have been lowered into the sea from surface ships. Recently, a lively debate took place within the government concerning the effort, if any, which should be taken to send men to the greatest depths of the ocean—some 35,000 feet. The arguments pro and con were similar to those now being used in connection with the man-in-space program. On the one hand, devices which will permit men to descend to great depths are very expensive. Perhaps the same amount of money invested in surface ships and in high-quality instrumentation would, in the long run, yield more information about the ocean's depths than could possibly be obtained by sending men down in a thick steel sphere. On the other hand, man himself is an instrument far more complicated, and

from certain points of view more effective, than those built in factories.

No matter what parameter one might be interested in, it is vitally certain that an instrument can be made which is more accurate than a
human being. A man can estimate temperature, but not as accurately as
a thermometer. He can look at a rock and estimate its chemical and min-
eralogical composition, but instruments are available which will do the
job much more accurately. However, the human brain can integrate observations in terms of a broad over-all pattern. A man-built machine
which could do this as well as a human being would be both unbelievably complex and expensive.

Let us imagine the geology of North America being determined
entirely by remote control. It seems clear that we would know far less
than we actually now know as the result of detailed human participation,
and particularly as the result of human competence with respect to the
integration of observations. Or, to take another example, what would
the scientific productivity of the voyage of the *Beagle* have been if a
series of measurements had been substituted for Charles Darwin?

The importance of man as an integrator and sifter of information
should not be underestimated. Yet, we should recognize that we are as
yet far from the point where such capability can be utilized effectively
in the space program. For each dollar of expenditure, far more useful
information can be obtained at the present time from instruments than
from men. But we would be cold, indeed, were we to take the point of
view that our every action must be justified by practical results or by the
gleaning of specific scientific information. In particular, we should not
ignore the man-in-space program as a great human adventure.

We spend very large amounts of money on games and, closely related
to them, adventure. Last year about twenty million persons attended
major league baseball games, and gross receipts at motion picture thea-
ters exceeded one billion dollars. Is two or three billion dollars a year
too much to pay for space adventure? One may argue about the magni-
tude of the space effort in the United States, and one may well argue
about the proper distribution of that effort. But no matter how we look
at the program, it seems clear that the adventure component must be
recognized. The first non-stop flight over the Atlantic gleaned little
information of scientific value. Yet, that first flight was important from
several points of view, not the least of which was the adventure aspect.

The budget for the American space effort has risen from about ninety
million dollars in 1958 to about 3.7 billion dollars for the National
Aeronautics and Space Administration alone in 1963. NASA projects

that expenditure will take place at a rate of about thirteen billion dollars annually by 1970. Today the space program consumes over twenty per cent of the total governmental research and development effort. By 1970, it is estimated, space projects will take up nearly forty per-cent of the research and development budget. Considering the technical difficulties, even these large numbers may prove to be underestimates, particularly if past military experience can be taken as a guide.

The greater part of the current space allocations is for the man-in-space program. With a current budget of 2.2 billion dollars, this program is already receiving about two-thirds of the total space agency allotment, and even now there are signs that the manned space program is running short of money. According to present estimates, the Apollo project (the first manned lunar landing) will be at least 200 million dollars short of its needs with its current budget. Without a supplemental appropriation, the only way to make up the deficit will be to take money away from other programs, such as the space sciences. Yet, there is already evidence that the space sciences are not providing information sufficiently rapidly to fill the needs of the manned space program.

Thus far, and in spite of the large sums of money involved, the pursuit of space technology has received overwhelming support from American political leaders. The basis for this support is complex, but it is clear that it was triggered by the national humiliation received on October 4, 1957, when Sputnik I was launched successfully. Subsequent Soviet space successes, particularly in the manned-space-flight area, have served to strengthen American resolve to achieve leadership in this field. In addition to the Cold War aspects of space, there is undoubtedly a feeling for the drama and adventure of conquering the unknown, and a desire to achieve practical applications. But were the Cold War element suddenly removed, it is dubious that space projects would receive the enthusiastic support which they enjoy today.

The general public does not appear to be as enthusiastic about space as its leaders are. Indeed, a number of professional people, including some prominent scientists, have expressed their doubts about the wisdom of pursuing such a program. There are numerous signs of a latent uneasiness. There are even some signs of direct hostility.

A large part of the uneasiness concerning the space program probably stems from the fact that so much money is being spent on an effort which has little obvious bearing upon the major problems which confront our nation and the world today. People who are rightfully concerned about hunger in the world cannot help thinking of how much economic development could be stimulated with 3.7 billion dollars this year, growing rapidly to thirteen billion dollars by 1970. People who are rightfully worried about the alarming rate of population growth in the world cannot help thinking of what 3.7 billion dollars might do if directed toward the solution of that problem. Educators think of how much education could be purchased, and worry about the effect of the influx of space-designated funds upon the intellectual values of their staffs and students. Others argue that large expenditures on space hinder the allocation of funds to other branches of science, to social science, and to the humanities. It seems possible that this uneasiness, which has been expressed in many different ways, will permeate American political leadership in the not-far-distant future.

The political fact of the matter, however, is that if space programs were completely eliminated, allocation of the funds for other worthy public purposes would not by any means be certain. In other words, the question of the emphasis we place on space projects should be decided on the intrinsic merits of the projects and not by comparison with other projects which might, in actual fact, be more useful.

The first question which we must answer is from many points of view the most difficult. Do we really want to venture into space? My own answer is an enthusiastic "Yes," but I would like us to go into space for the right reasons and not for the wrong ones. We should venture into space simply because it is an enormously exciting thing to do. What is human destiny if it is not to learn about the universe in which we live? Americans should not engage in space projects simply because the Russians are engaging in them. I believe that the question of space in relation to "national prestige" is greatly overemphasized.

Can we afford to venture into space? At present, space expenditures do nat appear to be alarmingly high. Even at the rate of expenditure projected for 1970, the cost would come to less than two per cent of the American gross national product. This represents something like three to five per cent of the activity of the industrial sector of the economy. Indeed, it may well be that the funding of space activities represents an appreciable contribution to economic growth.

Given the desirabliity of venturing into space and given further the estimate that we can afford it, are we going about it in the right way? My personal feeling is that the Americans and Russians have been looking at space exploration primarily as a race, and in doing so have permitted themselves to become stampeded. In their push to place men on the moon as quickly as possible, they have inflated the man-in-space project to the point where it already dominates the space effort and threatens to envelop it.

Before we attempt to place men on the moon and planets and return them to the earth, we should study the objects as carefully as we can with instruments. By all means, we should aim at eventually sending men to the moon and planets, but we should take care of first things first. Should a Russian land on the moon first, it would not be a catastrophe for America. Indeed, we should recognize that no matter how much effort is placed on the manned-space-flight program, the probability is substantial that this will happen anyway. Also, the first man will probably not learn a great deal. The moon and the planets are large, and adequate exploration will require many lengthy visits. The establishmentt of the goal to place a man on the moon by the end of this decade makes a certain amount of sense, for it gives a definite time for a definite limited objective. But we should not permit our program to get out of balance, not should we permit it to become a circus just because such a goal exists.

Space experiments are, by their very nature, terribly expensive, with the result that they should be selected with the greatest possible care. It is often pointed out that the cost of a unit of information obtained in the space program is unreasonably high compared with costs of other areas of scientific inquiry. Here we must recognize that some bits of scientific information are by their very nature difficult to obtain. Nuclear physics has always been expensive, relative, let us say, to the study of butterfly ecology, largely because of the high cost of the equipment involved. Yet, we are willing to spend money on accelerators because we recognize that we cannot obtain the desired information unless we do so. Just as the jump from butterfly ecology to nuclear physics was expensive, so is the jump into space. We are confronted by the fact that we can obtain valuable information only if we are willing to spend the money. Unless we are willing to make a substantial (and expensive) effort, the information simply will not be forthcoming.

What are the conditions on other planets? Has life existed there in the past? Does it exist there today? To what extent does living intelligence permeate the universe? Can we contact it? Can we understand it? What is our past? Where lies our future? These are some of the questions which can be answered over the next decades and centuries through man's exploration of space. We are indeed on the threshold of the greatest of mankind's intellectual experiences.

NOTES

Robert Jastrow, *The Exploration of Space*, New York, 1960.
Hugh Odishaw (ed.), *The Challenge of Space*, Chicago, 1962.
George P. Sutton (ed.), *Advanced Propulsion Systems*, New York, 1959.
James A. Van Allen (ed.), *Scientific Use of Earth Satellites*, Ann Arbor, Mich., 1956.